Everyday Evangelism

Everyday Evangelism

Gareth Crossley

 EVANGELICAL PRESS

EVANGELICAL PRESS
16/18 High Street, Welwyn, Hertfordshire, AL6 9EQ, England

© Evangelical Press 1987
First published 1987

British Library Cataloguing-in-Publication Data:
Crossley, Gareth
  Everyday evangelism.
  1. Evangelistic work
  I. Title
  269'.2   BV3790

  ISBN 0-85234-239-X

Typeset by Alan Sutton Publishing
Printed in Great Britain by Cox & Wyman, Reading

To my best friend
for her partnership
in the gospel of Jesus Christ.

Contents

Prologue

Evangelism is a vast subject! In its simplest form, 'It is a work of communication in which Christians make themselves mouthpieces for God's message of mercy to sinners.'[1] Or, as Stuart Olyott expands this definition, 'Evangelism is the relating of the Evangel [Good News], by means of the spoken word, and in the power of the Holy Spirit – in order that men may seek God, repent of their sins, and believe on the Lord Jesus Christ and be saved; and then order the whole of their lives by his Word.'[2]

The church of today can no longer assume the right to speak to the unsaved about the great issues of life and death. We have to earn that right. Barging into the privacy of other people's lives shouting, 'Are you saved?' is not personal evangelism but would more appropriately be called impersonal evangelism. This form of 'attack' fails to respect the dignity and rights of all human beings – even the right not to believe in God! It is certainly contrary to the approach of the apostles, evangelists and Christians of the New Testament church. But furthermore, and of course more seriously still, such a method dishonours God. The Christian who behaves in this brash and insensitive manner salves his own conscience in supposedly fulfilling the commission to evangelize. Yet at the same time he probably hinders the cause of the gospel and makes true evangelization of his 'victims', at some future date, virtually impossible. There is a more excellent way. Appropriately it is the way of love and sensitivity. Let us remember where evangelism originates.

Evangelism began in eternity in the heart of God

The church is not engaged in a work *for* God so much as in a work *with* God. From the beginning his purpose has been not only to be merciful and compassionate in his attitude to sinners but also to ensure that sinners come to know and experience this aspect of his personality. At the very time of pronouncing punishment upon Adam and Eve for their terrible disobedience the Lord interwove with it a grand and glorious promise. To the serpent he said, 'I will put enmity between you and the woman, and between your seed and her Seed; he shall bruise your head, and you shall bruise his heel' (Genesis 3:15). The veiled promise of a Messiah, a Saviour, was introduced. That Seed of Eve was also later designated the Seed of Abraham through whom the Lord God would bless all the families and nations of the earth.[3] God fully intended that men should come to know him as a merciful God (Acts 17:26–27). His work of preparing for the arrival on earth of his only begotten Son was coupled with a constant seeking and calling men to salvation. God's evangelistic activity was somewhat restrained during the old covenant but the impact under the new covenant, from Pentecost onwards, is to be felt throughout the world.

Further evidence of God's work in evangelism is seen in the parables of the lost sheep, the lost coin and the lost son. God's compassion expresses itself in much searching and great personal inconvenience, in order to restore those who are lost. Couple the teaching of such parables with the heart-warming declarations of Jesus in John 10 and we have an indisputable picture of God not only going to tremendous trouble to make salvation possible, but also going to almost as much trouble to ensure that people come to benefit from it. The Lord Jesus came not only 'to give his life a ransom for many' (Matthew 20:28), but also 'to seek and to save that which was lost' (Luke 19:10). Christ is the Mediator/Evangelist. He is both the only sacrifice for sin and the Evangelist calling sinners to turn and live. Evangelism must always be seen in the context of God's working. It must be viewed from God's perspective. So it will be no surprise to any Christian reader that attention is first focused upon God's own activity.

God's evangelistic activity is not restricted to special efforts, campaigns or missions, nor are his agents restricted to special people like evangelists or ministers of the gospel. He has a much broader base for his working. Whether we appreciate the fact or not, every Christian is involved in evangelism. Many see evangelism as knocking on doors, giving out tracts or preaching in the open-air – and yet fail to see that the church assembling for worship has an evangelistic impact. Furthermore the Christian doesn't need to carry his Bible to work with him in order to be evangelizing. He doesn't need to be playing 'religious' records at home. His life is either attracting men, women and children to his Lord or it is putting them off. All Christians are witnesses for Christ – either good witnesses or bad witnesses. It is this diversity of God's evangelistic strategy which has prompted the writing of this book. Christian life itself is evangelistic – it paves the way for verbal communication in public preaching or in private conversation. Evangelism begins with God and passes through the warp and woof of church life in worship, prayer and fellowship. Through every believer impact is made – for good or ill. Naturally, some will be raised up to give themselves wholly to evangelistic enterprise. The church or churches will support them with prayer and finance, as was the practice in the early church. But whether through such recognized and supported believers or through believers who carry out their daily duties in work, home, church and community for the glory of God, Christ will build his church and sinners will be converted. Not one of us can claim any credit. To God be the glory!

> 'Not unto us, O Lord, not unto us,
> but to your name give glory,
> because of your mercy,
> and because of your truth . . .
> Our God is in heaven;
> he does whatever he pleases'
>
> (Psalm 115:1,3).

References:
1. J.I. Packer, *Evangelism and the Sovereignty of God*, IVP, p. 41.
2. Stuart Olyott, 'What is Evangelism?' *Banner of Truth* magazine, July-August 1969, quoted by Roy Joslin *Urban Harvest*, Evangelical Press, p. 88.
3. Genesis 12:3,7; 18:18, cf. Galatians 3:16.

1

God at work!

It does not take long for believers to realize the severe limitations which exist when we try to share our faith. Knowing the gospel to be 'the power of God to salvation for everyone who believes' (Romans 1:16), the young convert naturally assumes that all he needs to do is speak of Jesus Christ and him crucified and all the world will turn and be saved! The lesson is soon learned that we are quite powerless. We have not the ability to open blind spiritual eyes. We are unable by our pleading and persuading to break the power of Satan over a man's life. We cannot give life to those who are spiritually dead. Nor can we hope to convince sinners of the truth of the gospel by patient explanation. There is no possibility that we shall move men to obey the gospel by any of our warnings. There is not even the slightest possibility that one person should turn to God because of what we say or do. Those who receive Jesus Christ and believe in his name are born 'not of blood, nor of the will of the flesh, nor of the will of man, but of God' (John 1:13). When the gospel seems so clear and plain, so utterly convincing to us, it is difficult

to come to terms with the spiritual blindness of sinners all
around us. Why do they not see? We are soon forced to
reckon with the power of the evil one! As the apostle Paul
states, 'If our gospel is veiled, it is veiled to those who are
perishing, whose minds the god of this age has blinded,
who do not believe, lest the light of the gospel of the glory
of Christ, who is the image of God, should shine on them'
(2 Corinthians 4:3–4).

It is not simply an inability to put the facts clearly and
convincingly which severely limits us. Thank God we
have men who can express the gospel in clear and lucid
terms. Yet they would be the first to acknowledge their
limitations. Jim Packer pinpoints the problem: 'Regarded
as a human enterprise, evangelism is a hopeless task. It
cannot in principle produce the desired effect. We can
preach, and preach clearly and fluently and attractively;
we can talk to individuals in the most pointed and
challenging way; we can organize special services, and
distribute tracts, and put up posters, and flood the
country with publicity – and there is not the slightest
prospect that all this outlay of effort will bring a single
soul home to God'.[1]

Or, in the words of Scripture,

> 'This is the word of the Lord to Zerubbabel:
> "Not by might nor by power, but by my Spirit,"
> says the Lord of hosts' (Zechariah 4:6).

Consider the vision of the golden lampstand and the two
olive trees (Zechariah 4:1–7). The prophet saw a lampstand with a bowl on the top, having seven lamps. Each
lamp had seven feeding tubes. These forty-nine tubes
were connected to two olive trees which, by means of their
clusters of olives, produced a constant flow of oil to the
lamps. The prophet wants to understand the meaning of

the vision and after some delay he is told. 'It conveys the truth that in carrying on the work of the Church, it is not by human power that it is either to be advanced or retarded, but by the strength of God.'[2]

The lampstand represents the church of God, showing her mission to be a light-bearer in a dark world.[3] The material, gold, suggests her purity, preciousness and indestructibility. The seven lamps and seven times seven tubes indicate the many and varied ways in which light is to be given out. Yet at the same time they remind us of the many different ways in which God will supply the necessary grace. The olive trees represent the source of that grace, the Spirit of God, from whom come forth all supplies of strength for the church. Zerubbabel may have had only few visible resources but he had an inexhaustible supply of grace from the Lord. God is constantly whispering in the ears of his children, 'My grace is sufficient for you, for my strength is made perfect in weakness' (2 Corinthians 12:9).

In all this we need always to remember who God is. He is Lord over all. He created all things. He sustains all things. He brings all things into being. He disposes of his creation as he sees fit. And he evangelizes where and whom he will. It should be no surprise to us that God is sovereign! 'He does according to his will in the army of heaven and among the inhabitants of the earth. No one can restrain his hand or say to him, "What have you done?"' (Daniel 4:35.)

All Christians believe in the sovereignty of God. Every time a Christian prays he is acknowledging God's sovereignty! Indeed there is no point in prayer if the Lord God is weak or limited in his activity. If God were in any way impotent one could only hope for a good outcome; there would be no value in praying for it. The real power of prayer is based upon the real power of God! Furthermore there is no security to faith if God's purpose can be thwarted by human indifference or devilish interference. What would come of our Lord's promise: 'My sheep hear my voice, and I know them, and they follow me. And I give them eternal life, and they shall never perish; neither shall anyone snatch them out of my hand'? (John 10:27–28.) What confidence would we have in such words if our God were not all powerful and one who achieves 'all things according to the counsel of his will'? (Ephesians 1:11.) Thanks be to God, he is the Almighty – neither man nor devil is ultimately able to thwart his will. Nor would any Christian wish it otherwise.

Sovereignty and predetermination in evangelism

Predetermination means simply that something is determined, planned and decided beforehand. God has a predetermined course of action. He has made up his mind. He has carefully considered the situation and decided upon a particular course of action.

We know from Scripture that God predetermined the crucifixion of his Son Jesus Christ 'before the foundation of the world' (1 Peter 1:20). Peter actually expresses this fact in his sermon at Pentecost: 'Men of Israel, hear these words: Jesus of Nazareth, a man attested by God to you by miracles, wonders, and signs which God did through him in your midst, as you yourselves also know – him, being delivered by the determined counsel and fore-knowledge of God, you have taken by lawless hands, have crucified, and put to death . . .' (Acts 2:22–23).

Later, after the trial before the Sanhedrin, the early Christian church quoted Psalm 2 and then prayed with great earnestness: 'For truly against your holy Servant

Jesus, whom you anointed, both Herod and Pontius
Pilate, with the Gentiles and the people of Israel, were
gathered together to do whatever your hand and your
purpose determined before to be done' (Acts 4:27–28). It
is interesting to note the form of address that they used
for the Lord on that occasion. They prayed, '*Despota*,'
'Sovereign Lord', 'Absolute Ruler' (Acts 4:24). In human
rulers the word 'despot' has become linked with op-
pression and tyranny because human beings are always
tainted with selfishness and sin. They cannot generally
exercise such authority without corruption. But God is
God. He is the Lord of all. He is also unspeakably 'good'.
He alone is perfect in goodness! 'No one is good but one,
that is, God' (Matthew 19:17). We should submit
thankfully to his kingly rule. For it is sheer arrogance on
our part to suppose that we can tell God what he is to be
like and how he is to behave: 'Indeed, O man, who are you
to reply against God? Will the thing formed say to him
who formed it, "Why have you made me like this?"' Does
not the potter have power over the clay . . . ?' (Romans
9:20–21.)

Not only does the Scripture teach clearly that the death
of Jesus Christ was predetermined by God; it also teaches
equally clearly that our salvation was predetermined by
God. Our Lord was 'the Lamb slain from the foundation
of the world' (Revelation 13:8). So also God 'chose us in
him before the foundation of the world, that we should be
holy and without blame before him in love' (Ephesians
1:4).

Predetermination and predestination are understandable activities of a sovereign God. While it should be no
surprise to us that God is sovereign it should be a great
surprise to us that God is so gracious. What kindness,
what love, what compassion, what grace, God shows to his
children! God's almighty power chooses to express itself

in the greatest love story of all time. Calvary love is so
potent and unselfish that all other loves pale to insignificant emotions in the light of it.

Paul states the position clearly and emphatically as he
writes to the Christians at Ephesus: 'Having predestined
us to adoption as sons by Jesus Christ to himself,
according to the good pleasure of his will . . . in whom
also we have obtained an inheritance, being predestined
according to the purpose of him who works all things
according to the counsel of his will' (Ephesians 1:5,11).

Which is the more surprising, that God should be
sovereign over his whole creation, or that he should be so
unspeakably generous to some of his human creatures? It
is truly amazing that God should use his wisdom and
power to open the blind eyes of men to see and
understand their self-imposed darkness and ruin; that
God should use his sovereign grace in defeating our
former vile master, Satan; that God should shower his
mercy, compassion and overwhelming love on sinners
who well deserve an eternal hell. Whatever intellectual or
emotional difficulties may be aroused by the truth of
God's sovereignty, his undoubted grace and mercy should
melt the heart into adoring praise!

God's sovereignty is no cold, cruel thing! 'Look to me,
and be saved, all you ends of the earth! For I am God, and
there is no other' (Isaiah 45:22). The Lord God issues a
genuine heartfelt invitation to all men to turn to him and
live. His sincere invitation to all 'assures them that
nothing would please Him more than their acceptance of
His offer'.[4] We have only to turn to such well-known
Scriptures as the following: 'For God so loved the world
that he gave his only begotten Son, that whoever believes
in him should not perish but have everlasting life' (John
3:16); '"As I live," says the Lord God, "I have no pleasure
in the death of the wicked, but that the wicked turn from

his way and live. Turn, turn from your evil ways! For why should you die?" (Ezekiel 33:11.) 'God our Saviour . . . desires all men to be saved and to come to the knowledge of the truth' (1 Timothy 2:4). 'The Lord is not slack concerning his promise, as some count slackness, but is longsuffering towards us, not willing that any should perish but that all should come to repentance'; as well as other Scriptures, such as Ezekiel 18, which contradict the conclusion that God is unfeeling or callous.

God's sovereignty and human responsibility

This issue is constantly raising its head in Christian circles. How can we harmonize God's sovereignty with human responsibility? Great volumes have been written in an attempt to reconcile these irreconcilables. Some want to place the emphasis upon God's sovereignty. Others would place the emphasis upon human responsibility. It comes as a great relief to realize that we are not intended to reconcile, by human logic and reason, that which to humans is irreconcilable.

Antinomy

Jim Packer designates the problem as an antinomy. An antinomy is 'a contradiction between conclusions which seem equally logical, reasonable or necessary'. Being logical is not the main object of our faith. We must be *theo*logical first and foremost! The being of Jesus Christ as the God-man is not logical; it is theological. The doctrine of the Trinity is not logical, it is theological. The Lord says, 'For my thoughts are not your thoughts, nor are your ways my ways . . . For as the heavens are higher than the earth, so are my ways higher than your ways, and my thoughts than your thoughts' (Isaiah 55:8–9). And so it is with the vital matter of salvation and human respons-ibility. God saves – or we are not saved. It is his work. To him belongs all the glory. His predestined will is the determining factor in the evangelizing of the world. 'For whom he foreknew, he also predestined to be conformed to the image of his Son, that he might be the first-born among many brethren. Moreover whom he predestined, these he also called; whom he called, these he also justified; and whom he justified, these he also glorified' (Romans 8:29–30; cf. Acts 13:48). 'He chose us in him [Christ] before the foundation of the world, that we should be holy and without blame before him in love, having predestined us to adoption as sons by Jesus Christ to himself, according to the good pleasure of his will . . .' (Ephesians 1:4–5).

Human responsibility is expressed, for example, in the lament of the Lord Jesus: 'O Jerusalem, Jerusalem, the one who kills the prophets and stones those who are sent to her! How often I wanted to gather your children together, as a hen gathers her chicks under her wings, but you were not willing!' (Matthew 23:37.) On another occasion Jesus warned the Jews that unless they repented they would perish (Luke 13:1–5). God 'now commands all men everywhere to repent, because he has appointed a day on which he will judge the world in righteousness' (Acts 17:30–31). God's emphasis upon human responsibility means that not one person will have an excuse when called before him on that great day.

God's sovereignty and human inactivity

Some unbelieving people on the fringes of church life grasp a totally wrong view of sovereignty. I have heard it said by some such people, 'I cannot believe, therefore I am not among the elect!' and 'I cannot save myself, therefore I will wait for God to do something!' C.H. Spurgeon, that oft-quoted champion of God's sovereignty and human responsibility, wrote, 'It is fatalism, not predestination, that makes men talk as if there is nothing whatever for them to do, or that there is nothing they can do.'[5] A wrong view of sovereignty produces such inactivity in unbelievers.

The same unbiblical and unbalanced view of sovereignty can also produce an equally wrong attitude in the converted. They conclude that there is no point in evangelism: 'God will save sinners in his way in his time. He doesn't need us. There is no value in speaking to unconverted people about the Lord!'

Since the temptation to think in such a misguided way is always a reality we need to be very clear and firm in our thinking on this theme. The Bible clearly teaches the following truths. Firstly, God is sovereign, and nowhere more so than in salvation. Secondly, man is responsible and nowhere more so than for his sin. Thirdly, the church is under commandment to make the gospel known: 'Go therefore and make disciples of all the nations . . .' (Matthew 28:19).

God is the great Evangelist. He is engaged in communicating his own message of mercy to sinners. God is sovereign. He rules the heavens, hell and the earth (and all that is beyond it). He has a predetermined plan. He knows what he is doing. He doesn't make mistakes. 'As for God, his way is perfect' (Psalm 18:30). The Lord is directing every process and ordering every event for the fulfilling of his own eternal plan. All Christians unite in the declaration of Paul, as having been 'predestined according to the purpose of him who works all things according to the counsel of his will' (Ephesians 1:11). We are not to make guesses about God's will nor to presume that we, in this day and generation, have prophetic insight: 'The secret things belong to the Lord our God, but those things which are revealed belong to us and to our children for ever, that we may do all the words of this law' (Deuteronomy 29:29). We have the revelation of God's will in Scripture. The Bible makes our duty and responsibility to evangelize as clear as crystal. God is the great Evangelist. We are privileged to share in his grand work.

Predetermination – thank God!

Because of God's sovereignty all who are to believe will believe. As the Lord says, 'I am God, and there is no other; I am God, and there is none like me ... My counsel shall stand, and I will do all my pleasure' (Isaiah 46:9–10). The pattern is set. The final outcome is beyond dispute. The church will grow. More sinners will be converted. As among the Gentiles at the first, 'as many as had been appointed to eternal life believed' (Acts 13:48), so it will be until the return of the Lord Jesus Christ (2 Peter 3:4–10).

Because of human responsibility all who do not believe condemn themselves. As Jesus said, 'He who believes in [the Son of God] is not condemned; but he who does not believe is condemned already, because he has not believed in the name of the only begotten Son of God' (John 3:18). None will be able to point the finger at God and blame him for their banishment into outer darkness.

Because of God's sovereignty evangelism is bound to succeed! There is this positive note running throughout the New Testament. When Christ sends out his church to evangelize the world he assumes success: 'All authority has been given to me in heaven and on earth. Go therefore and make disciples of all the nations' (Matthew 28:18–19). He does not commission his servants to failure but to success. All our evangelism hinges upon the Lord's authority. If he sends us forth it must be his will for us to succeed!

When God permits us to see conversions, we shall not be tempted to claim the credit because of our gifts, or skill, or wisdom, or persuasiveness. Knowing the Word of God and the clear teaching of God's predetermination and predestination we shall readily admit and acknowledge that it is his work and his work alone.

References
1. J.I. Packer, *Evangelism and the Sovereignty of God*, IVP, p. 109.
2. T.V. Moore, *Commentary on Zechariah*, Banner of Truth Trust, p. 72.
3. Matthew 5:14–16; Ephesians 5:8; 1 Peter 2:9; Philippians 2:15.
4. R.B. Kuiper, *God-Centred Evangelism*, Banner of Truth Trust, p. 182.
5. C.H. Spurgeon, *The Soul-Winner*, Pilgrim, p. 122.

— 2 —

The church at prayer

God is the great Evangelist. He knows what he is doing. Our responsibility is to fall in line with his plans. He can do his work without us. Our prayer should be that he will graciously use us. Knowing that the Lord has a predetermined plan and purpose and that he is actively engaged in directing the affairs of mankind towards his appointed end can cause two understandable reactions. The first is a fatalistic, 'There is nothing I can do,' sort of response. The second is the spiritual response, encouraged by the Lord through his Word – earnest prayer! The Christian reaction to God's sovereignty and to his predetermination is to pray. Part of God's predetermined plan is that his people should seek him, earnestly pray according to his revealed will and see their prayers wonderfully answered!

Effective prayer

We are told, in the context of a very practical matter, 'The effective, fervent prayer of a righteous man avails much'

(James 5:16). The prerequisite of such powerful prayer must not be overlooked. Only a righteous person 'praying in prayer' (as it is literally in v. 17) is effective and powerful in prayer. But there is a further point about Elijah's praying which James does not bring out in his letter. A careful study of the life of Elijah will reveal that he prayed according to the revealed will of God. The drought which is credited to Elijah's prayers in James 5:17 was specifically threatened by God through his servant Moses: 'Take heed to yourselves, lest your heart be deceived, and you turn aside and serve other gods and worship them, lest the Lord's anger be aroused against you, and he shut up the heavens so that there be no rain, and the land yield no produce, and you perish quickly from the good land which the Lord is giving you' (Deuteronomy 11:16–17).

King Ahab and his subjects were going to have ample opportunity to reflect upon the cause of this calamity. When Ahab was told of the punishment which was going to come upon the people there was no evidence of the truth of the prediction. The lush pastures, well-watered fields, the springs and the brooks flowing through the land – all these conspired to make nonsense of the prophet's words. Yet as time went on Ahab would have good cause to think. The word of the prophet struck like a fever into the heart of the earth, withering and scorching everything which was once fresh and green. The streams and brooks dried up and the earth began to crack open. Ahab must now take Elijah's words seriously. Ahab had many counsellors. In his desperation he had only to turn back to the Word of God for an answer, as Elijah had prayed in direct accord with God's promises.

Prayer principles

The three principles governing effective and powerful prayer as set forth in Scripture are:
1. Righteousness.
2. Real, earnest prayer.
3. Prayer according to God's will.
The first requirement is personal righteousness in the sight of God. Since Pentecost this righteousness is clearly linked with the persons of Christ and of the Holy Spirit. The requirement, therefore, is not only a confidence in the work of Christ ('the righteousness . . . which is through faith', Romans 3:22) but also walking righteously before God by his grace and in the power of the Holy Spirit (1 John 2:29).

The first and especially the last requirements are often overlooked. In a day when so many quote our Lord's words in John 14:12–14 in a superficial and careless manner, it is necessary to reassert the requirements for effective prayer. Verse 12 needs careful attention but is outside the scope of this book. Our concern here is for verses 13 and 14: 'Whatever you ask in my name, that I will do, that the Father may be glorified in the Son. If you ask anything in my name, I will do it.' This is not a 'blank cheque', signed by the Saviour, into which we can insert anything which takes our fancy! The Lord is not only encouraging prayer and 'asking'; he is putting down a condition. The prayer must be 'in his name'. This means far more than simply adding, 'in the name of Jesus Christ, Amen,' like a secret formula for success, at the end of all our prayers.

John clarifies and confirms the point in his first letter: 'Now this is the confidence that we have in him, that if we ask anything according to his will, he hears us. And if we know that he hears us, whatever we ask, we know that we have the petitions that we have asked of him' (1 John 5:14–15). This means that our prayers will only be answered as they are in line with God's own will. To pray in the name of Jesus Christ is exactly the same as praying in accordance with the will of God. It is not a lack of faith when we do not *demand* action and intervention; it is respect and reverence towards the one whom we address. In prayer we seek to tune ourselves to his will. We are admitting our inadequacy and calling upon the Lord to hear and answer, if it pleases him and if it is in perfect accord with his most holy will! 'Prayer . . . is a confessing of impotence and need, an acknowledging of helplessness and dependence, and an invoking of the mighty power of God to do for us what we cannot do for ourselves.'[1]

Lack of evangelistic zeal

When we feel deserted and alone, bewildered and confused, the only thing which will lift the heart and cheer the spirit is a view of God's working among us. Hence the last two verses of Psalm 90 are appropriate:

> 'Let your work appear to your servants,
> and your glory to their children.
> And let the beauty of the Lord our God be upon us,
> and establish the work of our hands for us;
> yes, establish the work of our hands'
>
> (Psalm 90:16–17).

As Leupold comments, 'In the last analysis these verses offer the potent and effective antidote against hopelessness and discouragement. They raise the eyes of him who prays this from the puny and ineffective work that man toils over down here on earth to the great and successful work that God does both here and in heaven. The trouble with man all too frequently is that he sees nothing of the work God is doing . . . that work which from the point of view of our most urgent concern is the work of the salvation of mankind.'[2]

For a child of God to be unaware of what God is doing is one great cause of utter hopelessness. When we do not glimpse something of the success of God's work, no wonder we become so easily despondent and depressed! Thus this prayer is so essential: 'Let your work appear to your servants.' This is followed by further clarification, in typical Jewish parallelism: 'And your glory to their children.' We really see the glory of God in a most powerful and effective way when we see just how marvellously he does his work!

Seeing God at work!

'God alone has the overall, eternal strategy at his fingertips. While he may not direct us in this era through visions, angels or audible voices, nevertheless we must be no less attentive than were the apostles to the direction of the divine Strategist. He may direct us where our common sense would tell us not to go . . . God compelled Philip to go to the Ethiopian, Peter to the Roman, and Paul to go across to Macedonia.'[3]

> 'A man's heart plans his way,
> but the Lord directs his steps' (Proverbs 16:9).

> 'There are many plans in a man's heart,
> nevertheless the Lord's counsel – that will stand'
> (Proverbs 19:21).

Knowing God's will

The discerning of the will of God requires the reading, study and meditation of the Scriptures. Here we learn the will of God. Through God's Word we learn not only how to pray but also what to pray. An example of how to pray is given in the Sermon on the Mount in what is commonly called 'the Lord's Prayer' but should more correctly be called 'the disciples' prayer' (Matthew 6:9–13). Some biblical examples of subjects for prayer may be helpful at this point.

Subjects for prayer, 'According to God's will'

1. We are to pray *for an understanding of God's will for us* – to be able to see him at work and share in his labour. Our constant prayer should be 'Let your work appear to your servants, and your glory to their children' (Psalm 90:16).

2. We are to pray *that God would work in us* 'both to will and do for [or, to work on behalf of] his good pleasure' (Philippians 2:13), so that the promise might be fulfilled in us: 'Your people shall be volunteers in the day of your power; in the beauties of holiness' (Psalm 110:3). A readiness to be flexible and available is incumbent upon all Christians. The writer to the Hebrews concludes his letter with a prayer that God may 'make you complete in every good work to do his will, working in you what is well pleasing in his sight, through Jesus Christ, to whom be glory for ever and ever' (Hebrews 13:21).

3. We are to pray *for success* in all evangelistic endeavours. As the apostle Paul urged the Christians at Thessalonica, 'Brethren, pray for us, that the word of the Lord may have

free course and be glorified, just as it is with you, and that
we may be delivered from unreasonable and wicked men;
for not all have faith' (2 Thessalonians 3:1–2). The Lord
can open doors for the gospel. Indeed we know our
Saviour is 'he who has the key of David, he who opens and
no one shuts, and shuts and no one opens' (Revelation
3:7). If he sets an open door before us, no one can shut it
(Revelation 3:8). The apostle Paul wrote to the Christians
at Colosse: 'Continue earnestly in prayer, being vigilant
in it with thanksgiving; meanwhile praying also for us,
that God would open to us a door for the word, to speak
the mystery of Christ' (Colossians 4:2–3). And when there
is danger of becoming 'weary while doing good' (Galatians 6:9), then let us 'wait on the Lord' that we might
renew our strength (Isaiah 40:31).

4. We are to pray *for more workers* to labour for the cause of
the gospel. As the Lord Jesus said, 'The harvest truly is
great, but the labourers are few; therefore pray the Lord
of the harvest to send out labourers into his harvest'
(Luke 10:2).

5. We are to pray *for boldness in speaking God's Word*. As the
early Christians prayed, 'Now, Lord . . . grant to your
servants that with all boldness they may speak your word'
(Acts 4:29). And look at the results which followed: 'And
when they had prayed, the place where they were
assembled together was shaken; and they were all filled
with the Holy Spirit, and they spoke the word of God with
boldness' (v. 31). 'And with great power the apostles gave
witness to the resurrection of the Lord Jesus. And great
grace was upon them all' (v. 33). Later, after the apostolic
discipline of Ananias and Sapphira, 'great fear came upon
all the church and upon all who heard these things' (Acts
5:11). These three 'greats' are still needed in our day. We

do not expect the doors and foundations to be shaken today, but we long to see 'great power' in the preaching of the Word of God; 'great grace' in the congregation of the saints and 'great fear' upon saints and sinners alike, so that God is honoured and reverenced, as is his right!

After urging the Christians at Ephesus to put on the whole armour of God 'and the sword of the Spirit, which is the word of God', the apostle Paul exhorts them to be 'praying always with all prayer and supplication in the Spirit . . . for all the saints – and for me, that utterance may be given to me, that I may open my mouth boldly to make known the mystery of the gospel' (Ephesians 6:18–19).

6. We are to pray, not only *for powerful preaching* of the Word of God, but also correct and accurate preaching of the Word of God. All teaching must be carried out with a due sense of reverence and seriousness. To every preacher the church should say, 'Be diligent to present yourself approved to God, a worker who does not need to be ashamed, rightly dividing the word of truth' (2 Timothy 2:15).

7. We are to pray *for blessing upon the church* as we worship the Lord. The same spirit of earnestness should be upon us as was upon Jacob when he wrestled with God! When Jacob struggled with the Lord all through the night he became a type of all true believers who would lay hold upon the Lord by faith. Let that same urgency and longing be ours: 'I will not let you go unless you bless me' (Genesis 32:26). Christians need to develop great earnestness in prayer and great perseverance too. George Müller knew much about persistent prayer. He wrote, 'The great fault of the children of God is that they do not continue in prayer – they do not go on praying; they do

not persevere. If they desire anything for God's glory, they should pray until they get it.'[4]

May the Lord shake us from lethargy in the matter of prayer: 'A little sleep, a little slumber, a little folding of the hands to sleep . . .' (Proverbs 6:10). We need patience and watchfulness in order to 'pray without ceasing' (1 Thessalonians 5:17). The Lord kept Abraham waiting twenty-five years for the fulfilment of the prophecy concerning the son of promise!

8. We are to pray that *'the beauty of the Lord our God be upon us'* (Psalm 90:17). The goal of our teaching and preaching within the church is for us all to 'come to the unity of the faith' and grow into that 'perfect man, to the measure of the stature of the fulness of Christ' (Ephesians 4:13). God's intention for his children is nothing less than our 'being transformed into the same image' and likeness to his only begotten Son (2 Corinthians 3:18). That work will be completed instantly at the Lord's return: 'When he is revealed, we shall be like him, for we shall see him as he is' (1 John 3:2).

9. We are to pray *for our children*. Oh, that they would see God's glory! Consider again Psalm 90, especially verse 16: 'And your glory to their children.' The disastrous afflictions which were hitting the Israelites were a grave burden upon the people. They cried out that God would show forth his gracious character. They longed for a display of God's goodness, God's power and God's grace, that this terrible evil would be halted and removed, so that their children could live and have reason to praise and bless the name of the Lord for the wonders of his love.

In our day we need to pray that God's glory may be seen by our children in the powerful demonstrations of conversions! Let it be known to this generation that

'The Lord's hand is not shortened,
that it cannot save;
nor his ear heavy,
that it cannot hear'

(Isaiah 59:1).

May it be that 'in the time of their trouble they will say,
"Arise [O, Lord] and save us" (Jeremiah 2:27). May all
our children know this 'so great a salvation' (Hebrews
2:3) as their own personal experience!

Now it may seem that much of this is not related to the
subject of evangelism. Some of the material is obviously
connected: prayer for open doors, for evangelistic success,
for conversions, for the raising up and sending forth of
evangelists and labourers into the harvest ... and so
forth. But you may wonder what worship and the beauty
of God upon his people have to do with evangelism. They
have considerable relevance. In the next chapter the
importance and place of worship in evangelism will be
established from Scripture. Later in the book great
emphasis will be placed upon the quality of Christian life
as being an important tool in the process of evangelism.

A brief summary

Evangelism begins in the heart of God. He wills to make
his mercy to sinners known in all the earth. God has
determined to save sinners. He planned the coming of his
only begotten and ever-beloved Son into the world. Even
before the foundation of the earth the triune God had
determined that, in order to uphold his good name and at
the same time save sinners from the consequences of their
sin, Christ Jesus should die as a substitutionary atonement. Every true believer can say,

Bearing shame and scoffing rude,
In my place condemned he stood;
Sealed my pardon with his blood:
Hallelujah! what a Saviour!

(Philipp Paul Bliss)

God knows what he is doing. He has the future all worked out. Our task is to learn his will, submit ourselves to his leading and get on with his work in his name and in his way.

Once there is a clear understanding that God is sovereign and has a predetermined will which he is bringing to pass, then prayer becomes an obvious reaction. The saints pray in order to know God's will. The saints pray to be useful to God in the fulfilling of his plans. The saints pray that God's holy will might be done on earth as it is so perfectly done in heaven (Matthew 6:10). There is also a further incentive to prayer: 'It is God who works in you both to will and to do for his good pleasure' (Philippians 2:13). In prayer the soul seeks that right 'willingness' to be granted by the Lord. He is not only the Giver of grace and gifts for the fulfilling of his purpose; he is also the Giver of the desire and willingness to work in the fulfilling of that purpose.

In the early church there was a continual dependence upon God. Believers expressed this in prayer. If it is God's will which we seek to be disclosed to us, rather than our will which we seek him to bless for us, then top priority in the church will be given to the matter of prayer. This is God's ordained means for the establishment of a good, sound, working relationship. To know his will we need to seek his face. We so much need his help. We need the Holy Spirit to remove the veil from our eyes so that we can see Christ clearly in the Scriptures (2 Corinthians 3:16–18). How apt is the prayer of Psalm

119:18: 'Open my eyes, that I may see wondrous things from your law'! The Bible will be a dead book without the Holy Spirit's illumination. Putting the teaching and commandments of the Scriptures into practice will be impossible without this divine assistance. So too, evangelism will be a futile exercise if we have not the 'Breath of heaven'.

References
1. J.I. Packer, *Evangelism and the Sovereignty of God*, IVP, p. 122.
2. H.C. Leupold, *Exposition of Psalms*, Baker, p. 648.
3. Eric Wright, *Tell the World*, Evangelical Press, p. 74.
4. George Müller, *George Müller, Man of Faith*, Warren Myers, p. 9.

— 3 —

Believers going to worship

Worship and evangelism

While it can readily be seen that prayer has a vital part to play in evangelism – and I am sure all Christians are agreed upon the necessity for much intercession – it is not always recognized that worship as a whole plays a distinct part in the evangelistic process. Before we examine this point in detail we need to establish the clear relationship between dynamic worship and the health of the church. By 'dynamic' I mean 'active, potent or energetic' – not to be confused with noisy, uncontrolled or superficial! 'Dynamic' is a good word to use for Christian activity as it is derived from the Greek *dunamis*, which is used on numerous occasions to describe the powerful activity of God[1]. Furthermore the gospel itself is declared to be the 'power [lit. dynamic] of God to salvation' (Romans 1:16; cf. 1 Corinthians 1:18; 1 Thessalonians 1:5). By the term 'dynamic worship' attention is drawn to the presence and power of the Holy Spirit in worship. The promise of the

Lord Jesus Christ is often quoted: 'Where two or three are
gathered together in my name, I am there in the midst of
them' (Matthew 18:20), but often we are not conscious of
that presence.

Unfortunately worship is not always dynamic, real and
full of meaning. Far too often it is dull, empty and
repetitive. In such services the unconverted could be
forgiven for believing that God is dead! John Miller
quotes a friendly visitor who attended a church service
and commented afterwards, 'I agreed with the theology of
the sermon, but the whole service carried the odour of
death.'[2] Sadly this comment could be applied to a number
of churches up and down our land. Doctrinal accuracy has
often gone hand in hand with spiritual deadness! What a
disaster! The opposite should be the case. True doctrine
should produce dynamic and vital worship. The two
should be wedded inseparably together. (Even in the
churches and 'fellowships' where there has been a total
swing to 'open' worship and modern songs, activity has
been mistaken for life.)

What is worship?

'The light of nature shows that there is a God who has
dominion and sovereignty over all. He is just and good,
and He does good to all. He is therefore to be feared,
loved, praised, invoked, trusted and served by men with
all their heart and soul and strength. But the only
acceptable way of worshipping the true God is appointed
by Himself, in accordance with His own will. Consequently He may not be worshipped in ways of mere
human contrivance, or proceeding from Satan's sug-
gestions. Visible symbols of God, and all other forms of
worship not prescribed in the Holy Scripture, are

expressly forbidden.'[3] Erroll Hulse, commenting upon this paragraph in the *1689 Confession of Faith* writes, 'This principle of regulation is far-reaching in its effects. It does not only prohibit, circumscribe, limit and restrain, but it also liberates ... because it frees God's people from innovations.'[4] Leaders in the church are able to use the clear principles of Scripture to remove unbiblical practices, just as the Reformers used them to purify the church.

The Christian converts on the Day of Pentecost 'who gladly received [Peter's] word were baptized ... and they continued steadfastly in the apostles' doctrine and fellowship, in the breaking of bread, and in prayers' (Acts 2:41–42). Their new relationship in the church of Jesus Christ expressed itself in united worship. 'Though they had been suddenly converted, though suddenly admitted to the church, though exposed to much persecution and contempt, and many trials, yet the record is that they adhered to the doctrines and duties of the Christian religion.'[5]

No aspect of collective worship should be stressed to the detriment of the others. While preaching is an important and indispensable part of worship it must not be elevated to a position of superiority. Such an elevation of preaching with the resultant playing down of prayer, Scripture reading and singing (often lumped together under the dishonouring term 'the preliminaries') may have greatly contributed to the swing over to 'praise and prayer' meetings with their emphasis on worship without preaching!

The presence of God in worship

Singing, the reading of Scripture, prayer and preaching, coupled with baptism and gathering around the Lord's

Table, are the ingredients of worship. But these activities can be engaged in without any expression of spiritual life and dynamic. It is as though Elijah had built the altar, cut up the bullock and prayed – and yet no fire had fallen from heaven!

In the early Christian church there was a continual sense of the presence of God. The believers expressed this in their worship. 'Worship must precede work, and prayer precede programmes, if sterility, frustration and fruitlessness are not to result.'[6] To put it another way, spirituality precedes strategy. The result of priorities given to worship and prayer will be that as we become God-oriented in our devotional life we shall become God-directed in our evangelism. We must pray for the blessing of the Lord that his name be glorified, his truth be upheld and his living presence experienced as we worship the Lord together.

The importance of collective worship for the health of the church

'Behold, how good and how pleasant it is for brethren to dwell together in unity'(Psalm 133:1), and nowhere more so than when they are collectively at worship. As believers we must not forsake 'the assembling of ourselves together, as is the manner of some' (Hebrews 10:25). The Lord takes particular pleasure in the collective worship of his people (Psalm 87:2). He is pleased to meet with his people as they worship. Only one response is fitting for the King of kings: 'I will praise the Lord with my whole heart, in the assembly of the upright and in the congregation' (Psalm 111:1). 'With my whole heart' – that is, with undivided affection, holding nothing back, allowing no distraction, no coldness, no love for other things, no unbelief, no distrust of the Lord or of his providential care. I will permit nothing to be in my heart which would interfere with the fulness of praise for the living God!

The collective benefit of public worship should not be overlooked. We do not come as individuals to worship God. Such individual worship is right and proper in the privacy of our own home. Rather when the church assembles something extra occurs. It is a true expression that 'A group is more than the sum of its individual members,' and this is especially true of the church group. Herbert Carson, in his stimulating book on Christian worship, writes, 'When we gather in a local congregation we are to realize that we belong together. We are not simply a group of like-minded people who meet together in a similar fashion to members of some club or guild. We have been united by the life-giving power of the Holy Spirit to the body of Christ. As such we are not only in living union with the Head but in organic union with each other. A healthy body is one in which all the limbs function harmoniously under the direction of the brain. An injury to the nervous system can produce uncontrolled spasms or varying degrees of paralysis. So the body of Christ is to function under the direction of Christ with the life of the Spirit reaching into each limb of His body. The frenzy of mere religious excitement, or the sluggish and moribund reactions of some congregations, are alike evidence of a lack of submission to the Head of the church, and to the direction of the Spirit.'[7]

The importance of worship in evangelism

Generally speaking, evangelism is divorced from most other aspects of church life. It is often isolated to a small group of keen believers who are left largely unsupervised and unsupported. What is worse is that few believers realize the importance of worship itself in evangelism.

A church with a concern for evangelism often falls into the trap of putting on 'special' meetings where great care is taken to have lively hymns (or choruses), a short address ('mustn't call it a sermon') and a real warmth of welcome during the meeting and afterwards. What a contrast when interested or even converted people then decide to visit the church for 'normal' worship! That same church is lifeless. The hymns are often dreary. The sermon is now much longer and in an unknown tongue (as used in Britain 350 years ago) and the visitor is utterly bewildered. When no one speaks to him after the service he leaves thoroughly disillusioned.

Before any effective evangelism is undertaken the church must set its own house in order. If worship is dull and dreary with long and irrelevant preaching and if no concern and interest are expressed towards the visitors, then evangelism might as well be forgotten!

Evangelism is to be the concern of the whole church. Spiritual people engaged in dynamic relevant worship are a magnetic attraction to the unbeliever!

The prophecy of Zechariah 8:20–23

> 'Thus says the Lord of hosts:
> "Peoples shall yet come,
> inhabitants of many cities;
> the inhabitants of one city shall go to another,
>   saying,
> 'Let us continue to go and pray before the Lord,
> and seek the Lord of hosts.
> I myself will go also.'
> Yes, many peoples and strong nations

shall come to seek the Lord of hosts in Jerusalem,
and to pray before the Lord.'

'Thus says the Lord of hosts: 'In those days ten men
from every language of the nations shall grasp the
sleeve of a Jewish man, saying, 'Let us go with you,
for we have heard that God is with you'
(Zechariah 8:20–23).

'God is with you.' What a reputation for a church to
have in the community! In Zechariah 8:20–23 we see the
church gathering for worship: 'Let us continue to go and
pray before the Lord, and seek the Lord of hosts' (v. 21).
What a blessing if men and women of the world, neighbours, friends, workmates and family should grasp hold of
our arm and plead with us, 'Let us go with you, for we
have heard that God is with you'! (v. 23.) This prophecy
keeps the priority clearly before our minds. The attraction
is not the superb singing, fine preaching or the social
concern expressed by the church; it is rather the
awareness of something unique about that church. That
church, whatever its shortcomings in other respects,
knows the reality of God's presence!

Our united worship is one of the ways in which the
reality and power of the living Christ are shown to the
world. Such a gathering of God's people is no ordinary
fellowship. Here God meets with his people in heavenly
fellowship. A living and dynamic church is by its very
nature evangelistic. People must take notice. A living
church cannot be ignored.

May the Lord God make his presence so real in our
meetings for prayer and worship that the word will get out
among the unconverted. May God grant that people of
different races and nations might be stirred in their hearts
to seek the Lord and pray to him. May we hear over and

over again the entreaty: 'Let us go with you, for we have
heard that God is with you.' And may they too grasp the
sleeve of the great Jew, Jesus of Nazareth, and by living
faith come to know him in truth to be 'the Christ, the
Saviour of the world' (John 4:42).

References
1. God's eternal dynamic is demonstrated in creation –
   Romans 1:20.
   God's dynamic activity raised Jesus Christ from the dead
   and will raise us also – 1 Corinthians 6:14.
   God's dynamic assures our preservation – 1 Peter 1:5.
   God's dynamic gave us all things that relate to life and
   godliness – 2 Peter 1:3.
   Christians abound in hope through the dynamic of the Holy
   Spirit – Romans 15:13.
   Signs and wonders were performed through God's dyna-
   mism – Romans 15:19.
2. C. John Miller, *Evangelism and Your Church*, Presbyterian and
   Reformed Publishing Company, p. 3.
3. *A Faith to Confess*, The Baptist Confession of Faith of 1689
   rewritten in modern English, Carey Publications Ltd. p. 50
   section 1.
4. Erroll Hulse, *Reformation Today*, Magazine No. 70, November
   – December 1982, p. 4.
5. Albert Barnes, *Notes on the Acts of the Apostles*, Routledge,
   p. 57.
6. Eric Wright, *Tell the World*, Evangelical Press, p. 100.
7. Herbert M. Carson, *Hallelujah! Christian Worship*, Evangelical
   Press, p. 42.

Now a new period has dawned. As our Lord informed the woman of Samaria, 'Woman, believe me, the hour is coming when you will neither on this mountain, nor in Jerusalem, worship the Father ... The hour is coming, and now is, when the true worshippers will worship the Father in spirit and truth; for the Father is seeking such to worship him. God is Spirit, and those who worship him must worship in spirit and truth' (John 4:21,23–24).

Unbelievers in our congregations

People may come to worship because a friend has invited them. Others come because members of their family are involved. Some may come because they have seen a number of folk entering the premises each Sunday and they are simply curious. Strangers may come because they see our publicity. Individuals may come because they are lonely. Those whose lives have been shattered by disease, divorce or death may turn to the church in desperation. Disillusioned and unhappy people may come because they have lost all sense of meaning and purpose to life. Where are confused human beings to turn if they cannot turn to the Christian church? So there are one hundred and one reasons why visitors appear in our congregations. What do we most want for them? We want a divine confrontation, a meeting with God himself! The desire is for a personal encounter to take place. We want each person, man, woman or child, to be confronted by the living God. This confrontation is not confined to the preaching alone, but includes the genuine welcome at the door, the warm environment of the church, the awareness of the sincere worship of believers on every side, the heartfelt singing of sensible hymns and spiritual songs,[2] understandable prayers, the serious and careful reading

of Scripture and, particularly, the sense of the presence of
God. The reality of the whole experience may then be
crystallized in the proclamation of the gospel.

When the Holy Spirit confronts the unbeliever through
the reality of Christian worship that man is stirred to join
in. He worships the Lord. The impact produces the
results stated in 1 Corinthians 14:25: 'Thus the secrets of
his heart are revealed; and so, falling down on his face, he
will worship God and report that God is truly among you.'
This verse is most helpful in showing how God, at times,
works evangelistically through worship. The text falls into
four natural sections. However, before we consider these
words in more detail it is necessary to consider the
context. We must not make the error of tearing a
convenient text out of its rightful place in the Bible. As
with all verses of Scripture it must be used only in the way
and manner in which it is intended. Otherwise the Bible
will be made to look foolish and teaching will have no
solid and concrete foundation upon which to build. Let us
look, then, at the context of 1 Corinthians 14:25.

Intelligent and intelligible worship

Irrespective of what view is held with regard to the
continuation or cessation of the special spiritual gifts, one
thing at least can be agreed upon. Paul was arguing for
intelligent and intelligible worship. Unintelligible worship, as, for example, speaking in a foreign language
without translation (or in our own day, using complex and
archaic phrases), is not helpful to the church (v. 5). The
Lord places a considerable emphasis upon the use of the
mind, but the mind can only be involved when the
vehicles of communication, the words, are understandable. It is not only the believing members of the church

who suffer. Those who come in unconvinced about the faith will not be challenged, convicted and converted unless they understand what is going on. Seekers and strangers (the uninformed and the unbelievers, respectively, v. 23) will be positively hindered. They will soon form the conclusion that Christians are mad!

The whole of our worship must be intelligible. We are to confront each visitor's intelligence with the living Word of God so that 'the secrets of his heart are revealed'. The worship of God is not an irrational activity. Luther's vivid caricature, 'that old witch lady reason', was not a condemnation of reasonable faith, reasonable preaching or reasonable worship. Far from it. He was decrying the attitude of placing reason above Scripture in the determination of truth. He would tolerate neither the 'church' nor 'reason' as being the authority for Christian belief and behaviour. The Bible stands alone. Here is the only authority for faith and practice. Yet, having said that, there is need for the use of the mind in understanding the Scriptures. Meditation upon God's Word (Psalm 1:2) requires much mental activity.

Three effects are ascribed or credited to intelligible worship – conviction, examination and revelation. *Conviction* is when a man is convinced of error or sin. *Examination* is when a man's whole mind and soul are searched out. Many a man and woman have sat under preaching and felt as though the preacher had inside information – detailed knowledge of their past and of their sins in particular! *Revelation* is when the sinner sees his condition in the sight of a holy God, as did Peter when he cried out,'Depart from me, for I am a sinful man, O Lord!' (Luke 5:8).

Or again in the words of Job,

> 'I have heard of you by the hearing of the ear,
> but now my eye sees you.

Therefore I abhor myself,
and repent in dust and ashes' (Job 42:5–6).

1. The secrets of his heart are revealed

God reaches the heart through the mind and conscience.
Romans 6:17 puts the issue most clearly: 'God be thanked
that though you were slaves of sin, yet you obeyed from the
heart that form of doctrine to which you were delivered.'
They were set free from their slavery to sin by the activity of
the will, that is, by obedience. This obedience came from
the heart, the seat of the emotions. By reversing the order
we see the process of the Holy Spirit's working in bringing
a sinner to gospel faith. The mind is informed through the
teaching or doctrine declared. Receiving and believing
the truth causes a reaction in the heart. Once we believe
the good news that God has sent his Son into the world
'that the world through him might be saved' (John 3:17),
and that 'Christ Jesus came into the world to save sinners'
(1 Timothy 1:15), it is then a natural reaction to love God.
The sinner's heart is stirred and enlivened to achieve its
finest emotion – love for the living God. 'In this is love, not
that we loved God, but that he loved us and sent his Son to
be the propitiation for our sins' (1 John 4:10). 'We love him
because he first loved us' (1 John 4:19).

Any attempt to bypass the mind brings dishonour to
God's cause. His invitation is 'Come now, and let us reason
together!' (Isaiah 1:18); 'Gird up the loins of your mind, be
sober . . . ' (1 Peter 1:13). It is only through the renewing of
our mind that we are able to 'prove what is that good and
acceptable and perfect will of God' (Romans 12:2).

While it is important to win the heart and persuade the
will, evangelism is ineffective if the mind or intellect is
bypassed. If the mind is not won, the person is not won. It is

not necessary to be a psychologist to know that the
feelings may be manipulated by specially chosen music
and singing. Certain hymns will most certainly bring an
emotional response. The true meaning of the words may
not be understood but excitement can be aroused. (A
vivid illustration of this fact is the singing of 'Abide with
me' at the annual Cup Final.) Emotions can be stirred
with the aid of special lighting effects. More seriously
still, the heart may be assaulted by tear-jerking details
and vivid verbal portrayals of the scourging and
crucifixion of Christ. The Bible is strangely brief in its
account of these experiences of our Lord. .What great
temptation exists for the preacher to embellish the
record by a detailed description of the whip with its
strips of leather, sharp-pointed bones or pieces of metal
fastened to the ends, etc!

In the Scriptures the most horrific events relating to
our Saviour's atoning work are simply stated without
detail. Indeed there is a glaring understatement: 'So
then Pilate took Jesus and scourged him' (John 19:1).
And again, 'When they had come to the place called
Calvary, there they crucified him . . . ' (Luke 23:33). The
reason behind such simple statements, which lack
detailed description, is not hard to find. Most human
hearts can be stirred by a vivid account of human
suffering. We naturally empathize with the pain of our
fellows. But the Lord Jesus Christ does not want our
pity. He wants our worship! When carrying the cross
Jesus said to the women mourners by the roadside,
'Daughters of Jerusalem, do not weep for me, but weep
for yourselves and for your children' (Luke 23:28). The
emotions of pity and compassion can be stirred by the sight
of human suffering. We are to encourage men to see
through the suffering to the God-man who went willingly,
voluntarily to his own execution, that they may adore

him, worship him and yield to him. Worship is his due:

> 'Worthy is the Lamb who was slain
> to receive power and riches and wisdom,
> and strength and honour and glory and blessing'
> (Revelation 5:12).

Preaching Jesus Christ and him crucified (1 Corinthians 2:2) is not to be aimed at creating a sense of pity but rather a sense of worship, adoration and praise.

A direct assault upon the will, in preaching, is offensive. Preaching can so easily deteriorate into a verbal blasting of the will. Crude psychological pressure can be exerted upon a congregation. A verse of a hymn can be repeated over and over again (I have heard of a verse being repeated as many as ten times!). Claims can be made such as, 'There is someone here resisting God. Yield to him. We shall not go home until you do!' Such tactics should be outlawed as vile perversions of gospel ministry, yet they are not uncommon experiences. The intention is to browbeat the will into submission. It is assumed that where the right end is achieved (supposed or actual yielding to God) then the method is justified. The Lord, however, does not use such an approach. Preachers who profess to serve him ought not to stoop to such a level either.

Worship should be an important part of the true response to God in fulfilment of his will: 'You shall love the Lord your God with all your heart, with all your soul, *with all your mind*, and with all your strength' (Mark 12:30).

2. Falling down on his face

No one ever received mercy on his feet! A great sinner freely pardoned bows in the dust before his King! 'Falling down on his face' (1 Corinthians 14:25) is an apt description of a humbling work of God. Confronted with the glory of God, his righteousness, power and might, taught about the grace of God as it is so beautifully and powerfully revealed in 'Jesus Christ and him crucified'(1 Corinthians 2:2), the convicted sinner cries out,

> 'Have mercy upon me, O God,
> according to your lovingkindness;
> according to the multitude of your tender mercies,
> blot out my transgressions.
> Wash me thoroughly from my iniquity,
> and cleanse me from my sin' (Psalm 51:1–2).

When Isaiah saw a vision of the Lord God Almighty he cried out,

> 'Woe is me, for I am undone!
> Because I am a man of unclean lips,
> and I dwell in the midst of a people of unclean lips;
> for my eyes have seen the King,
> the Lord of hosts' (Isaiah 6:5).

Humility is the mark of the man who realizes he is in the presence of the living God. Without humbling there is no repentance. Without repentance there is no true faith. Without conviction there is no conversion. No one will walk into heaven with his head held high, thinking what a fine man he is. Nebuchadnezzar learned humility the hard way (Daniel 4:32). He became like an animal walking on all fours, eating grass. Thank God when he humbles you. 'God resists the proud, but gives grace to the humble' (James 4:6; cf. Proverbs 3:34). 'Godly sorrow produces repentance to salvation' (2 Corinthians 7:10).

3. He will worship God

The effects of conviction upon unbelievers result in their joining in the worship of God. Rebellion and unbelief express themselves in a disregarding of God. The evidence of his being and glory are present all around in nature (Romans 1:20). Even within the human brain there is inscribed a testimonial to the Creator (Romans 2:15). Only 'the fool has said in his heart, "There is no God"' (Psalm 14:1). In spite of the testimony to God present in the whole creation and in their consciences, because of the hardness of their hearts, men still refuse to bow in worship. 'Although they knew God, they did not glorify him as God, nor were thankful, but became futile in their thoughts, and their foolish hearts were darkened' (Romans 1:21). Paul's analysis of his day is equally well suited to our own. Men know God yet refuse to acknowledge him and to give thanks and worship.

4. And report that God is among you

If worship is the converted sinner's response in the assembly then testimony is his response outside the assembly. When confronted by the presence of the living God a man will not have to be told to tell others. There will be no wish to keep the experience to himself. It will be like Matthew, who invited his old friends to meet the Lord Jesus Christ (Luke 5:29). Like the woman of Samaria who rushed back to the city of Sychar, after meeting with the Lord Jesus Christ, those who are converted in the worship service will want to share the news (John 4:29).

When the early Christians were driven from Jerusalem under persecution we read, 'They were all scattered throughout the regions of Judea and Samaria. . . Therefore those who were scattered went everywhere preaching the word' (Acts 8:1,4). Wherever these Christians were driven by persecution and harassment they shared the good news of Jesus Christ. 'These were ordinary Christians; they did not set themselves up as preachers but told people why they had to leave Jerusalem and thus testified to their faith in Christ Jesus. They fulfilled the duty that is to this day incumbent on every Christian.'[3]

The testimony of the man converted in worship is 'God is truly among you' (1 Corinthians 14:25). In the past such enthusiastic reporting has resulted in whole households coming to faith in Christ. May the Lord grant more enthusiasts!

> My heart is full of Christ, and longs
> Its glorious matter to declare!
> Of him I make my loftier songs,
> I cannot from his praise forbear;
> My ready tongue makes haste to sing
> The glories of my heavenly King.
>
> (Charles Wesley)

References

1. The term 'church community' is used to describe the group of believers and unbelievers who gather together. The 'church' is strictly those who are born of God, have repented of their sins and believed on the Lord Jesus Christ for salvation.
2. A careful choice of 'psalms, hymns and spiritual songs' (Colossians 3:16) will avoid the meaningless repetitions and highly emotional material to which this generation is all too prone.
3. R.C.H. Lenski, *The Interpretation of The Acts of the Apostles*, Augsburg Publishing House, p. 314.

5

Preaching in the assembly

An essential ingredient of church worship is the preaching of the Word of God. The new Christians converted on the Day of Pentecost 'continued steadfastly in the apostles' doctrine' as well as in 'fellowship, in the breaking of bread, and in prayers' (Acts 2:42). The Word of God has to be handled carefully and taught accurately (2 Timothy 2:15). The Word of God is the Scriptures which are not only 'able to make . . . wise for salvation' but are totally inspired and ensure 'that the man of God may be complete, thoroughly equipped for every good work' (2 Timothy 3:15–17). This is why we are to give respect and honour to those who 'labour in the word and doctrine' (1 Timothy 5:17).

No spiritual person would question the value and necessity of the exposition of God's Word in the assembly of believers. However, what is often questioned is whether evangelistic preaching should be conducted in the church assembly. This naturally raises two questions: what is evangelistic preaching, and should it be done in the church?

Evangelistic preaching

Christians often speak of 'preaching the gospel', but it is
not always clear what is meant. Many of the Puritans
identified 'preaching the gospel' with preaching 'the
whole counsel of God' (Acts 20:27). Others, particularly
in our own day, mean by 'preaching the gospel' a presentation of limited truth surrounding the cross of Christ.
Often, on the basis of 1 Corinthians 2:2 ('I determined
not to know anything among you except Jesus Christ and
him crucified') the ingredients would be as follows:
something taught about God's holiness and righteousness, sin explained and identified, the sacrificial
death of Jesus Christ presented and a direct challenge
issued to the hearer.

Preaching the gospel is preaching the Word of God as
'good news'. This can be done to saint or sinner. Indeed,
the Word of God, in all its variety of subjects, should
always come to Christians as 'good news'. Regrettably the
gospel can be preached in such a way that it is not
preached evangelistically! It is good news only to those
who understand it. When, however, the language,
thought forms, expressions and illustrations are beyond
the experience and understanding of unbelievers, then
although the gospel is being preached it is not being
preached evangelistically. It will not convince an
unbeliever. Unconvinced unbelievers remain unconverted! Church 'lingo' may be as confusing and bewildering
as the foreign languages of New Testament times (1
Corinthians 14:23).

For our purposes here it may be helpful to get away
from this expression 'preaching the gospel' because of
confusion as to its meaning, and use instead 'preaching
evangelistically'. (The etymology of 'gospel' and 'evangelistic' would not allow this distinction but common

usage will.) Preaching evangelistically is preaching which is intended to address the good news directly to the unconverted! It is preaching 'the whole counsel of God' with particular reference to the unbeliever. If this is borne in mind then *all* preaching may have an evangelistic aspect to it. The vast majority of biblical truths have some evangelistic application – a challenge, a rebuke, an invitation, a warning, a confrontation, etc. In most cases this can be done without the slightest strain to the text.

Evangelistic preaching in the church

Should the Word of God be preached evangelistically in the church? The church of Jesus Christ is composed of believers alone. 'The word church properly means those who are called out, and is applied to Christians as being called out, or separated from the world.'[1] Strictly speaking the term 'church' should be used exclusively to denote converted persons, adults and children. If a preacher could be sure that there were no unconverted persons present in the congregation then evangelistic preaching would be out of place! However, no preacher can ever know the true spiritual state of the congregation. – Are there no unbelievers present? What about the children of believers? Are they all converted? We cannot be sure that all who profess faith are actually true believers. Our Lord's parable of the wheat and tares (Matthew 13:24–30,36–43) teaches that Satan has his counterfeits who can so easily be mistaken for real wheat! We expect Satan to have such counterfeits even in the gatherings of the Lord's people. Evangelistic preaching may be the very means the Lord will use to change these devilish tares into wholesome wheat! Evangelistic preaching will always be needed in the assembly! As Charles

Bridges pointed out, 'The church as well as the world needs a quickening ministry.'[2]

The Christian preacher is under obligation to preach the good news. It is his life's work. It is no ground for boasting. As Paul says, 'Necessity is laid upon me; yes, woe is me if I do not preach the gospel' (1 Corinthians 9:16). The Word of God is to be preached as good news – to saint and to sinner. In this respect every preacher must be ready and willing 'to do the work of an evangelist' (2 Timothy 4:5). The man who preaches in the church assembly without an evangelistic thrust and application is not being true to his calling as a Christian preacher! The discharge of Timothy's responsibilities meant an application of God's Word to both saint and sinner. So Paul writes, 'Take heed to yourself and to the doctrine. Continue in them, for in doing this you will save both yourself and those who hear you' (1 Timothy 4:16). Preaching in the assembly may be likened to a twelve-bore double-barrelled shot gun. One barrel is for the believer – applying God's Word to those in the faith. The other barrel fires application at the unbeliever – to challenge, convince and convert.

One of the great exponents of this dual approach to preaching, C.H. Spurgeon, spoke of his overriding aim: 'I would sooner bring one sinner to Christ than unpick all the mysteries of the Divine Word, for salvation is the one thing we are to live for.'[3]

Preaching Christ

Every sermon ought to draw sinners to Christ and establish Christians in their faith. The very sermon which presents Christ as Lord and Saviour for conversion is the means of consolidating the believer. 'Nothing but the truth of the Gospel can be instrumental to the conversion of souls. Any wilful suppression – or any compromising statement of truth, dishonours the Holy Spirit in his own special office, and therefore restrains his quickening influence. Many earnest, affectionate, and diligent Ministers are mourning over the palpable unfruitfulness of their work; without at all suspecting, that the root of the evil lies within themselves.'[4] When the apostle Paul declared his determination to know nothing among the Christians at Corinth 'except Jesus Christ and him crucified', he was not thereby restricting his preaching to the issues surrounding the cross. 'Paul's only design in going to Corinth was to preach Christ; and Christ not as a teacher, or as an example, or as a perfect man, or as a new starting-point in the development of the race – all this would be mere philosophy; but Christ as crucified, i.e. as dying for our sins. Christ as a propitiation was the burden of Paul's preaching. It has been well remarked that "Jesus Christ" refers to the person of Christ, and "him crucified", to his work; which constitute the sum of the gospel.'[5]

The preaching of Christ crucified has to be 'full and explicit. Let it comprehend within its circle the whole mystery of Christ, in his person, offices, and work; connected with the love of the Father, and the work of the Spirit, in every department of privilege, duty, promise, and hope.'[6] The Lord Jesus Christ is the grand subject of the Old Testament just as clearly and decisively as he is of the New. Like our Lord with the two disciples on the Emmaus Road, preachers should expound to the congregation 'in all the Scriptures the things concerning' Christ (Luke 24:27).

Jesus as Christ and Lord

'God has made this Jesus . . . both Lord and Christ,' says

Peter on the Day of Pentecost (Acts 2:36). In outlining the causes of failure in today's preaching Al Martin says one 'area where the content of our preaching is weak in specific application, is in the matter of presenting the whole Christ to the whole man'. People 'need to be brought to the understanding that saving faith involves the commitment of the whole man to the whole Christ as Prophet, Priest and King, as He is set forth in the gospel'[7].

Preaching Jesus Christ and him crucified is a vast subject. All the doctrines of Scripture relate in some way to the Saviour. When Christ is presented clearly and winsomely to unbelievers evangelistic preaching is in progress.

Preaching with a challenge

Evangelistic preaching addresses the unconverted or those with a nominal profession of faith. It carries with it a plea. There is no cold and dispassionate presentation of truth. The preacher puts his heart and soul into his work: 'We implore you on Christ's behalf, be reconciled to God' (2 Corinthians 5:20).

Jim Packer asks a question with regard to preaching: 'Is it going to make people think, and think hard, and think hard about God, and about themselves in relation to God?'[8] What we long to see is preaching owned and anointed by the Holy Spirit so that the hearers are 'cut to the heart' as on the Day of Pentecost under Peter's preaching that they may say, 'Men and brethren, what shall we do?' (Acts 2:37–38.) Or that they may cry out with the Philippian jailer, when confronted by the mighty working of the God of Paul and Silas, 'Sirs, what must I do to be saved?' With what delight will we reply, as they did,

'Believe on the Lord Jesus Christ, and you will be saved, you and your household'! (Acts 16:30–31.)

The truth is always addressed to the mind, as we saw in the previous chapter. Here the emphasis is upon the preacher's approach to his task. Dr Lloyd-Jones, commenting upon Romans 6:17, where the apostle says, 'But God be thanked that though you were slaves of sin, yet you obeyed from the heart that form of doctrine to which you were delivered,' observes: 'They have "obeyed", yes; but how? "From the heart". What was it made them do this, what was it moved their hearts? It was this 'form of teaching' that had been delivered to them. What had been delivered or preached to them was the Truth, and Truth is addressed primarily to the mind. As the mind grasps it, and understands it, the affections are kindled and moved, and so in turn the will is persuaded and obedience is the outcome. In other words the obedience is not the result of direct pressure on the will, it is the result of an enlightened mind and a softened heart. To me this is a crucial point.'[9]

Plain and simple

In order to present the truth clearly to the congregation a preacher must give diligence to study in order to present himself 'approved to God, a worker who does not need to be ashamed, rightly dividing the word of truth' (2 Timothy 2:15). Labouring in the Word is not achieved without considerable output of mental energy (1 Timothy 5:17). Presenting ourselves to God as living sacrifices is our 'reasonable service,' or as it can equally well be translated, our 'intelligent service of worship'.

It is not sufficient for a preacher to study Scripture; he must study people as well. If our preaching is to reach home to the heart via the minds of our hearers it must be understood clearly by them. Some may dismiss a concern for effective communication as trying to do the Holy Spirit's work for him, but their reaction would be without biblical warrant. Let such people stand and read the Scriptures in the original languages and see how 'blessed' their hearers are! Scripture has to be read, interpreted and applied today just as in the days of Ezra and Nehemiah. In those days Ezra brought out the Book of the Law of Moses and he and his assistants 'read distinctly from the book, in the Law of God; and they gave the sense, and helped them to understand the reading' (Nehemiah 8:8).

Paul explained his straightforward and uncomplicated approach at Corinth:

'My speech and my preaching were not with persuasive words of human wisdom, but in demonstration of the Spirit and of power, that your faith should not be in the wisdom of men but in the power of God' (1 Corinthians 2:4–5).

That great evangelistic preacher John Wesley made a commitment to be clear and lucid in his preaching: 'I design plain truth for plain people: therefore, of set purpose, I abstain from all nice and philosophical speculations; from all perplexed and intricate reasonings; and, as far as possible, from even the show of learning, unless in sometimes citing the original Scripture. I labour to avoid all words which are not easy to be understood, all which are not used in common life; and, in particular, those kinds of technical terms that so frequently occur in Bodies of Divinity; those modes of speaking which men of reading are intimately acquainted with, but which to common people are an unknown tongue.'[10]

The preacher's task is to remove the stumbling-blocks of unbelief and self-righteousness to crush the unbeliever's reliance upon good works; the free and gracious invitations of Christ must be portrayed clearly; the willingness and ability of Christ Jesus to save must be established; his sufficiency to save to the uttermost, in terms of degree and of eternity, must be made clear; the certainty of the acceptance of all who repent and believe the gospel must be made known. Let all hear our Saviour's words: 'Come to me, all you who labour and are heavy laden, and I will give you rest' (Matthew 11:28). And again, 'The one who comes to me I will by no means cast out' (John 6:37).

Our subjects are sufficiently simple: sin and salvation; ruined man recovered by Jesus Christ. But it is of main importance that the sinner's way to Christ, like those to the cities of refuge under the old covenant, should be made plain.

Making contact

Haddon Robinson draws out the major concerns in effective preaching: 'The effectiveness of our sermons depends on two factors: what we say and how we say it. Both are important. Apart from life-related, biblical content we have nothing worth communicating; but without skilful delivery, we will not get our content across to the congregation.'[11]

All Christians must be familiar with the preacher who insists on looking into the top corner of the room while he is preaching. The congregation could slip out quietly, one by one, and the preacher would never notice! Haddon Robinson insists upon the necessity of 'eye-contact' between preacher and the members of the congregation: 'Eyes communicate. They supply feedback and at the same time hold an audience's attention. When you look directly at your hearers, you pick up cues that tell you whether they understand what you are saying, whether they are interested, and whether they enjoy the sermon enough to continue listening. An alert speaker will adjust what he says – for example, adding explanation or illustrations – as he interprets these responses. Moreover listeners feel that ministers who "look them in the eye" want to talk with them personally. Therefore pastors who gaze over the audience's heads, stare down at notes, look out of windows, or, worse, shut their eyes while they speak, place themselves at a crippling disadvantage. Almost without exception a congregation will not listen attentively to a speaker who does not look at them while he talks.'[12] If this is so vitally important when addressing Christians how much more so when speaking to the unconverted! Preachers behave too often as though they have a captive audience. Their preaching style and delivery are so dull and uninteresting that it takes a great deal of effort for the Christian to listen to them. The unconverted have no such patience or commitment.

Evangelistic preaching in the congregation aims to attract attention, grip the hearer and communicate the glorious truths concerning Jesus Christ. By open statements of the truth we commend ourselves 'to every man's conscience in the sight of God' (2 Corinthians 4:2). Our words are not adequate to express the true glory and majesty of Christ – after all is said and done he is God's 'indescribable [or, unspeakable] gift' (2 Corinthians 9:15). But, by the grace of God, we will try our utmost to bring the truth clearly before the minds of all who hear.

The glory and splendour of the Lord Jesus Christ is so great and commendable that surely no one can hear of him without melting in adoring worship and praise. Yet thousands hear and fail to respond. Thank God we have an explanation for this phenomenal blindness. If our gospel is hidden, it is hidden from 'those who are perishing, whose minds the god of this age has blinded, who do not believe, lest the light of the gospel of the glory of Christ, who is the image of God, should shine on them' (2 Corinthians 4:3–4). Satan has blinded their eyes!

The Holy Spirit's unique work

When the preacher has done his best to communicate the Word of God to the unbelievers present in the assembly, it will not be enough. The unconverted cannot understand the glory of the gospel until they are 'born again' or 'born of God' (John 3:3; 1:12–13). For the unbeliever cannot grasp the truths of the gospel (1 Corinthians 2:14), until God gives specific commandment for light to shine in his heart 'to give the light of the knowledge of the glory of God in the face of Jesus Christ' (2 Corinthians 4:6).

When Paul preached evangelistically at Thessalonica the Holy Spirit was graciously and powerfully at work both in the transmission of the gospel and in its reception. Paul was conscious of the Spirit's presence and working as he preached: 'Our gospel did not come to you in word only, but also in power, and in the Holy Spirit and in much assurance . . .' He sees also the Holy Spirit at work in his hearers: 'You became followers of us and of the Lord, having received the word in much affliction, with joy of the Holy Spirit' (1 Thessalonians 1:5–6). To put it in a slightly different way, Paul knew the subjective reality of the Holy Spirit's working even while he preached. He was therefore convinced of their election (v.4). He also knew the objective reality of the Holy Spirit's working in the Thessalonians receiving the Word and becoming disciples of Christ.

The Holy Spirit uses means. It is 'through the foolishness of the message preached' that God is pleased to save sinners (1 Corinthians 1:21). It is 'through the word of God which lives and abides for ever' (1 Peter 1:23) that sinners, 'dead in trespasses and sins,' 'having no hope and without God in the world' (Ephesians 2:1,12) are 'begotten . . . again to a living hope' (1 Peter 1:3).

Our Lord promised the arrival of the Holy Spirit in a new and dramatic way after his crucifixion. He outlined the unique work of this Spirit of truth: 'When he has come, he will convict the world of sin, and of righteousness, and of judgement: of sin, because they do not believe in me; of righteousness, because I go to my Father and you see me no more; of judgement, because the ruler of this world is judged' (John 16:8–11). The greatest sin of all is unbelief with regard to the Lord Jesus Christ. Only the Holy Spirit can enable a man to face up to this and admit his foolishness. We may speak of the breaking of God's commandments, either in the terms of the old covenant or of the new, but this ranks as the greatest offence of all – failure to believe in Jesus of Nazareth as Son of God and Christ of God: 'He who believes in him is not condemned: but he who does not believe is condemned already, because he has not believed in the name of the only begotten Son of God' (John 3:18).

The Holy Spirit also enables sinners to see the true nature of the Saviour. The Jews tried to malign the Saviour's name. The world blasphemes and dishonours the Lord. Through the grace given by the Holy Spirit we know and acknowledge the righteousness of the Lord Jesus. Once 'we esteemed him . . . smitten by God, and afflicted,' without realizing 'he was wounded for our transgressions, he was bruised for our iniquities' (Isaiah 53:34). Then we came to understand he was 'without sin' (Hebrews 4:15). Furthermore 'Christ also suffered once for sins, the just for the unjust, that he might bring us to God' (1 Peter 3:18). Such knowledge only comes by the enlightenment of the Spirit of God.

Anointed preaching

Evangelistic preaching to the unsaved within the congregation will only be effective when God wills. When the Holy Spirit made his presence felt in the early church there was 'great power' in preaching (Acts 4:33). The apostolic preachers not only 'spoke the word of God with boldness' (v.31), but they had an authority and clarity which convinced the people. So much so that 'believers were increasingly added to the Lord, multitudes of both men and women' (Acts 5:14). As we noted in chapter 2 in the matter of prayer, the presence and working of the Holy Spirit had three great impacts. There was 'great power' in the preaching, particularly concerning the resurrection of the Lord. Also there was 'great grace' among the people of God as they worshipped and fellowshipped together (Acts 4:33). Then there was 'great fear' in the church and community at large, following the disciplinary measures brought upon Ananias and Sapphira (Acts 5:11). When God the Holy Spirit demonstrates his presence among his people power, grace and fear – in very great measure – are seen and experienced.

The breath of heaven

The faithful evangelistic preacher declares,

> 'I have proclaimed the good news of righteousness
> in the great congregation;

indeed, I do not restrain my lips,
O Lord, you yourself know.
I have not hidden your righteousness within my
   heart;
I have declared your faithfulness and your
   salvation;
I have not concealed your lovingkindness and
   your truth
from the great congregation' (Psalm 40:9–10).

But all the people of God should be united in imploring
heaven, 'Come from the four winds, O breath, and
breathe on these slain, that they may live' (Ezekiel 37:9).

References
   1. Albert Barnes, *Notes on the Acts of the Apostles*, p. 60.
   2. Charles Bridges, *The Christian Ministry*, The Banner of Truth
       Trust, p. 246.
   3. Quoted by Percy O. Ruoff, *Personal Work*, IVP, p. 49.
   4. Charles Bridges, *The Christian Ministry*, p. 243.
   5. Charles Hodge, *A Commentary on the First Epistle to the
       Corinthians*, Banner of Truth Trust, p. 30.
   6. Charles Bridges, *The Christian Ministry*, p. 246.
   7. Al Martin, *What's Wrong with Preaching Today*, The Banner of
       Truth Trust, p. 18.
   8. J.I. Packer, *Evangelism and the Sovereignty of God*, IVP, p. 87.
   9. D. Martyn Lloyd-Jones, *Preachers and Preaching*, Hodder and
       Stoughton, p. 271.
  10. John Wesley's Preface, *Fifty-Three Sermons*, p. 3.
  11. Haddon W. Robinson, *Biblical Preaching*, Baker, p. 191.
  12. *Ibid*, p. 201.

—— 6 ——

Going out to make disciples

So far our whole attention has been focused upon what
God is doing in and through the church at prayer and
worship. We have noted that God is the great Evangelist
doing his own work and that much of his evangelistic
activity occurs in the assembled church. However, he is in
no way confined to such grouping. He is engaged out in
the world gathering people to himself. The Great Shepherd is searching for his lost sheep (Luke 15:4–6). He
knows each of his own and 'calls his own sheep by name'.
They recognize his voice and respond by following him
(John 10:3,14). God's patience is not to be considered as
slackness – God is not dilatory (2 Peter 3:9). He is in no
rush. The Lord has everything under control.

With or without the church

God can work through the church collectively or through
members individually. However, he can equally well

achieve his objective *without* the church. Inadequate, uncaring or lazy believers can no more jeopardize the growth of the body of Christ than can Satan from hell (Christ Jesus says, 'I will build my church, and the gates of Hades shall not prevail against it', Matthew 16:18). That typical missionary call, 'Unless you go to Africa and preach the gospel thousands will go to hell!' is not only totally untrue but it misrepresents God! No Christian could enjoy heaven if he knew that just one person languished in hell through his negligence. No Christian preacher could sleep soundly at night if he thought the eternal destiny of sinners rested upon his shoulders.

Thank God it is otherwise. The Saviour 'shall see the travail of his soul, and be satisfied' (Isaiah 53:11). Christ Jesus said with emphatic assurance, 'All that the Father gives me will come to me' (John 6:37). When this present age comes to a conclusion he will be able to say again to the Father, 'Of those whom you gave me I have lost none' (John 18:9).

We cannot hinder the growth of the church. Nor are we able to block the conversion of one human being. God does not need us to do his work. However, he allows us the privilege of working with him and for him. This is the context in which the Great Commission to the church is to be seen and understood. We shall look at it in detail.

The Great Commission

'All authority has been given to me in heaven and on earth. Go therefore and make disciples of all the nations, baptizing them in the name of the Father and of the Son and of the Holy Spirit, teaching them to observe all things that I have commanded you; and lo, I am with you always, even to the end of the age' (Matthew 28:18–20).

When considering these final instructions in evangelism which the Lord gave to the church attention is generally paid to the command 'Go' (Matthew 28:19). This has two effects. In the first place it is often presented in such a way as to deflect concern for evangelism to activity outside the gathered church, with the consequent neglect of the unconverted and nominal believers in the congregation. The second result is to highlight the activity of Christians without giving due consideration to the activity of Christ himself.

The commission is 'Go, therefore . . .' and the word 'therefore' brings into prominence the earlier words of Christ: 'All authority has been given to me in heaven and on earth . . .' (Matthew 28:18). Likewise, at the end of the commission, the assurance is given: 'Lo, I am with you always, even to the end of the age' (Matthew 28:20).

When a man is successful in business or public life credit is often given to the support and encouragement of his wife. The saying is, 'Behind every good man is a good woman,' or, 'Every good head sits on a good neck', the implication being that strength and support, behind the scenes, are an essential factor in successful achievements. In church growth the hidden support and strength is all important. Behind every successful evangelizing Christian there is the Great Evangelist. When the church evangelizes, Christ is evangelizing. The Lord is personally involved in the work and provides the necessary motivation, direction and authority.

The Lord earned the authority

It is interesting to note that the Lord gave this commission on a mountain. Three years earlier the devil had taken him up a mountain and shown him 'all the kingdoms

of the world in a moment of time'. The devil had made
Jesus an offer: 'All this authority I will give you, and their
glory; for this has been delivered to me, and I give it to
whomever I wish' (Luke 4:5–6). We know that the devil is
called 'the prince of the power of the air' (Ephesians 2:2),
or 'the ruler of this world' (John 12:31; 14:30; 16:11), and
we also know that 'the whole world lies under the sway of
the wicked one' (1 John 5:19). In offering the kingdoms to
the Lord Jesus Christ Satan was tempting him with a
compromise of authority and rule without the cross!
Christ Jesus had come to crush the enemy's head (Genesis 3:15), plunder his kingdom (Luke 11:20–22) and
liberate his captives by destroying the devil (Hebrews
2:14–15). Satan was here proposing an unholy alliance.
The Lord resisted such a suggestion and set himself to the
all-out warfare which would culminate in the final battle
on the cross!

The cost to the Lord Jesus Christ cannot be over-
estimated. An insight into the demands made upon him is
given in the prayer at Gethsemane: 'O my Father, if it is
possible, let this cup pass from me; nevertheless, not as I
will, but as you will' (Matthew 26:39), and also in that
nearly inexplicable cry from the cross: 'My God, my God,
why have you forsaken me?' (Matthew 27:46.)

The mountain after Calvary

Again on a mountain, but this time with the cross behind
him, the Saviour commissioned his church. Through his
sacrificial death, he had destroyed Satan's control. God
the Father had made Jesus, who was crucified, 'both Lord
and Christ' (Acts 2:36). He was 'highly exalted' and given
'the name which is above every name, that at the name of
Jesus every knee should bow, of those in heaven, and of

those on earth, and of those under the earth, and every tongue should confess that Jesus Christ is Lord, to the glory of God the Father' (Philippians 2:9–11). Christ 'must reign till he has put all enemies under his feet' (1 Corinthians 15:25).

Authority has been 'given', which obviously 'refers to the human nature of Jesus alone: for according to the divine nature all authority belonged to the Son from all eternity'.[1]

All authority in heaven and on earth

Christ has 'all authority *in heaven*'. All that lives and has its being there – angels and archangels, powers, principalities, might, dominion, thrones and the saints in glory – all are subject to Christ. All the powers of heaven are in his hand to do his bidding without question. The disciples are to realize this great fact as Jesus sends them out. Never has a human army had such resources behind it!

He has 'all authority *on earth*'. All its inhabitants – friend and foe and all the powers that are in the earth – all are subject to Christ. He has no limit to his authority. All the forces of nature, all the skills of man, are at his disposal and are to be harnessed for the spread of the glorious gospel. Theologians draw a distinction between Christ's kingdom of power and his kingdom of grace. The former is his universal power over all things. The latter is his headship over the church. Christ's kingly rule over the nations is exercised for the benefit of the church (Ephesians 1:10,20–23).

The church's work is Christ's work. He is in the midst of his church. In the language of the great revelation he stands 'in the midst of the . . . lampstands' (Revelation

1:13). He is also out in the world going up and down the nations 'conquering and to conquer' (Revelation 6:2).

When the Lord Jesus Christ has a purpose to extend his kingdom and enlarge his church he exercises sovereign rights. Even when saints in a local church, as at Philadelphia, are weak and struggling, by divine authority an open door is set before them, and no one can shut it (Revelation 3:8). Weak and impotent churches should look to the Saviour for the opening of doors so that the church of Jesus Christ might be gloriously extended.

An impossible task

We are sent into the world to do the things which humanly speaking are impossible. God delights to deal with these impossibilities. He works by his Holy Spirit through his believing people. When confronted by a hostile unbelieving world we might well ask, as the disciples of old, 'Who then can be saved?' Our Lord still gives the same answer: 'With men it is impossible, but not with God; for with God all things are possible' (Mark 10:26–27).

The words of the Lord in the Great Commission not only declare that the impossible is made possible; much more is implied. He is giving assurance of success. If our Lord Jesus Christ has *all* authority in heaven and earth, then the commission is given its impetus and force. We can press forward in absolute confidence. Because of our Saviour's divine backing and authorization we can 'be steadfast, immovable, always abounding in the work of the Lord, knowing that [our] labour is not in vain in the Lord' (1 Corinthians 15:58). Not only is the Christian able to cope with the general experiences of life, in either abundance or want, 'through Christ who strengthens' him

(Philippians 4:13), but he is able also to achieve all that Christ wants him to achieve in the world. The extension of the church is in the best possible hands – the hands of a sovereign Saviour!

'Be going . . .'

Going out to make contact with the unconverted is often viewed within very narrow confines. 'Outreach' is generally composed of such activities as open-air preaching, door-to-door visitation and the distribution of tracts, leaflets and invitation cards. Many Christians react in fear and trepidation when expected to participate in such things and needless guilt is caused. To define evangelism in these terms stifles and frustrates many of God's people by forcing them into a 'strait-jacket' unsuited to them. Furthermore, to expect people to come to meetings is to show partiality. Many people have insurmountable obstacles in their thinking about 'the church'. A combination of the institutional church and the media has effectively poisoned thousands of minds against Christianity. Most of our countrymen are not well disposed to come to a church service or meeting.

It is not uncommon for a church to distribute 25,000 leaflets inviting people to attend a gathering at which the good news is to be preached, and to find that not a single person responds! When a church has prayed hard and long in preparation for such a meeting it is all too easy for them to give up all such endeavours and rest content with a few unsolicited visitors who might come in through the year. Richard Baxter wrote, 'It is easy to separate from the multitude, and to gather distinct churches, and to let the rest sink or swim; and if they will not be saved by public preaching, to let them be damned: but whether this be the most charitable and Christian course, one would think should be no hard question.'[2]

Frank Tillapaugh has this advice for ministers of the gospel: 'Forget about bringing people in. Focus on getting God's people out where there is sin and pain and need.'[3] The irony is that many of God's people are out there already but are living such introverted lives that they make no real contact with other human beings. The Christian all too easily acts like an island and attempts to create as much expanse of water around him as possible. Churches behave like ghettos isolated from the rest of the world. 'The church is intended to be more like a guerrilla force than a fixed fortification.'[4]

Going out to make disciples, the evangelization of the nations, should occur on two levels. Firstly, men clearly called of God, with experience and proven skill, should be sent out and supported by the churches to work as evangelists. Secondly, all Christians should be living witnesses and should see their major evangelistic contribution as being constantly watchful and prayerfully ready to enter into any natural opening and opportunity to speak of the Lord Jesus Christ. Jim Petersen in his refreshing book *Evangelism as a Lifestyle* writes, 'God allows a certain division of labour in the ministry of reconciliation. Christians, individually and collectively, bear witness by their life and word. They bring the non-Christian within hearing range of the Scriptures. The Scriptures reveal the truth and testify of Christ. The Holy Spirit convicts, draws the person to repentance, and gives life ... Evangelism can be a normal and spontaneous aspect of our lives ... [being a living witness to Christ] is not limited to those with highly developed communication skills.'[5]

The difference of approach between the evangelist and other members of the church of Jesus Christ is quite distinct. Many Christians evangelize in the normal course of their lives without realizing it. A word in season in the office, factory, kitchen, or sports hall may be far more powerful than any sermon preached in the context of the church, and may be used of God to reach someone who would never have darkened the door of our meeting-place.

Christians are already out in the world, among the people, six days a week. The question is what are they doing there? Are they looking for the opportunity to make disciples? When the evangelistic work of the church is evaluated, whatever forms of outreach have been used, it will be seen that the majority of conversions come from one basic and common factor – Christian friendship. A believer somewhere, somehow, established contact, cared enough to take interest and show concern and introduced the person, directly or indirectly, to the Lord Jesus Christ.

All nations: all races

What a reaction must have been stirred up in the minds and hearts of those first Jewish disciples! They no doubt knew many of the Old Testament promises with regard to the bringing in of the Gentiles.[6] The Lord had taught them of this expansion of the kingdom.[7] They had heard Samaritans clearly confess, 'This is indeed the Christ, the Saviour *of the world*' (John 4:42). But to be commissioned to go out there to the non-Jewish nations was a direct assault upon their prejudice. Their reticence to go forth and proclaim the gospel to the nations had to be over-come in dramatic ways. In the providence of Almighty God persecution was to scatter the church throughout Judea and Samaria (Acts 8:1). Peter was to have a vision to help him over the hurdle (Acts 10:9–16). Gentiles were to experience the same outpouring as was granted to the

Jews at Pentecost (Acts 11:15–18). The universality of gospel proclamation was being reinforced. All nations were to be evangelized.[8] God had to give those first Jewish disciples more light and a few big pushes to get them moving out to the nations. God will have his way.

Making disciples of *all* nations places the church under a vast obligation. Christ Jesus will have a church which is multi-ethnic in composition. In many of our towns and cities a glorious opportunity exists. We have people from the nations right on our doorstep. Each local church should be a microcosm of the community in which it is set! The variety of peoples within the church is to reflect the vast variety of peoples outside the church (Ezekiel 47:10). What a rich blessing to be able to sing together of our Saviour, 'You were slain, and have redeemed us to God by your blood out of every tribe and tongue and people and nation'! (Revelation 5:9.) One day there will be that 'great multitude which no one could number, of all nations, tribes, peoples, and tongues, standing before the throne and before the Lamb, clothed with white robes, with palm branches in their hands, and crying out with a loud voice, saying, "Salvation belongs to our God who sits on the throne, and to the Lamb!"'(Revelation 7:9–10.)

'Make disciples'

Making disciples is far more involved than simply making converts. When people are converted, that is, when they are brought to the point where they confess with their mouths the Lord Jesus and believe in their hearts that God raised him from the dead (Romans 10:9), it is but the first stage in a long and exacting process. Much work might have been put in to arrive at this juncture but it is certainly not the end of the church's evangelistic

responsibilities. More time, energy and effort will be
needed to develop Christian discipleship. Discipleship
requires that a person not only comes to personal
commitment to the Lord Jesus Christ, as demonstrated in
baptism, but also that he goes on from there being
regularly instructed in the things of God and taught the
truth as it is in Jesus! (Ephesians 4:21.)

'Baptizing'

The place of baptism in evangelistic work needs careful
attention. How many evangelists ever mention baptism
when proclaiming the gospel and urging a response to the
person and work of Christ?

Following Peter's sermon at Pentecost, 'those who
gladly received his word were baptized' (Acts 2:41). True,
it is fair to assume that all these respondents were well
grounded in the truths of the Old Testament Scriptures.
They were, after all, 'Jews, devout men, from every nation
under heaven' (Acts 2:5). Consequently Peter's address
had built upon the solid foundation of accepted truth with
regard to the existence, nature and activities of the living
God. He did not need to argue the case for an inspired
Scripture. He argued from an accepted basis to prove that
Jesus of Nazareth was in fact the Christ of God and the
Son of God. When many within that vast congregation
responded readily with the cry, 'Men and brethren, what
shall we do?' Peter had no hesitation in responding,
'Repent, and let every one of you be baptized in the name
of Jesus Christ for the remission of sins; and you shall
receive the gift of the Holy Spirit' (Acts 2:38).

A similar situation existed with the Ethiopian minister
of state brought to faith in Christ through the agency of
Philip. It would appear he was already convinced of the

reliability of the Jewish Scriptures and sincerely wanted
to understand the meaning of Isaiah 53. Philip did what
any Christian evangelist would have done in his place: he
'opened his mouth, and beginning at this Scripture,
preached Jesus to him' (Acts 8:35). How long that
disclosure and discussion went on we are not informed
but the response of the Ethiopian was beyond question.
His question, 'See, here is water. What hinders me from
being baptized?' makes obvious that Philip had preached
Christian baptism to him as part of his message. What
vastly different replies this man would have received in
our own day! 'You must attend three months of "baptis-
mal classes", then if the church meeting votes in favour,
we will baptize you.' 'You must wait until there are clear
evidences of grace in your life. We want to see the marks
of conversion. We want to be sure that you are elect.'
'Don't rush into anything. Go home and think about all
that I have said and come back in a week or two and we
will consider baptizing you.' 'We shall have to go to the
church so that your baptism can be carried out by one of
the apostles or an ordained man and also before an
invited gathering of friends and neighbours as a public
declaration of your faith.' Philip had no such hesitation.
He said, 'If you believe with all your heart, you may.' And
he answered and said, 'I believe that Jesus Christ is the
Son of God' (Acts 8:37). And he was baptized.

Later in the development of the Christian church, as
outlined in the Acts, the position does not appear to
change. As the movement from the Jewish people to the
Gentile peoples gathered momentum the apostles were
increasingly confronted by people who had little or no
background knowledge of the inspired Scriptures. Yet
this does not seem to alter the immediacy of baptism. The
notable example of the Philippian jailer serves to illustrate the speed with which converts were baptized

following their profession of faith. He and his family were converted after midnight and baptized before breakfast! (Acts 16:25–34.)

We are under obligation to require penitents to be baptized – and the sooner the better. As God 'commands all men everywhere to repent' (Acts 17:30) so he requires of all who repent that they be baptized (Acts 2:38). A failure to preach baptism leaves penitents without a God-given means of visual, practical and immediate response. For many Christians there is considerable attraction in the 'appeal system' practised by many modern-day evangelists. The demonstrable response of walking out to the front in a meeting or signing a decision card is not to be dismissed out of hand as a trick to press unwilling people into the kingdom. Though this approach has been greatly abused at times, yet there is an underlying value in making a clear and decisive declaration of turning from the old life of sin to the new life in the Saviour. The appeal system has no biblical warrant or precedent. Baptism, when rightly preached and practised, is God's gift to the believer – an immediate, decisive, visual declaration of repentance and faith. It is in an instant 'the answer of a good conscience towards God' (1 Peter 3:21). Any delay between conversion and baptism will bring problems and lessen the value of this blessing to the believer. Let us preach, therefore: 'He who believes *and is baptized* will be saved' (Mark 16:16).

Teaching as part of the Great Commission

A mark of true conversion is continuing 'steadfastly in the apostles' doctrine' (Acts 2:42). The apostles' doctrine was the teaching of the correct interpretation of the Old Testament Scriptures combined with the teachings of the

Lord Jesus Christ which were clearly recalled to their
minds by the Holy Spirit (John 14:26). Later it was to
embrace new things revealed by the Spirit of truth (John
16:13; cf. 1 Corinthians 11:23; Revelation 1:1–2). In other
words, the baptized convert is to be taught the 'whole
counsel of God' (Acts 20:27), not with a view to head
knowledge alone, for that only creates arrogance (1
Corinthians 8:1), but with a view to obedience and
conformity. The Lord Jesus says, 'Go . . . teaching them
to observe all things that I have commanded you . . .'
(Matthew 28:20). Christ's laws alone are binding upon
the hearts and lives of his people. The church has no right
to insist on the observance of any other laws (Mark
7:6–13).

While our Lord places baptism before teaching in the
order of activity, it is clear that some teaching has to be
given before conversion is possible, and hence before
baptism is conducted. '"Whoever calls upon the name of
the Lord shall be saved." How then shall they call on him
in whom they have not believed? And how shall they
believe in him of whom they have not heard?' (Romans
10:13–14.) With the general decline in church
attendance, little or no Christian education in our
schools, non-attendance at Sunday Schools, the media's
constant undermining of and attack upon biblical
Christianity, coupled with modernism and liberalism
dominating most denominational pulpits, we go out to a
vast multitude who are almost entirely ignorant of the
teaching of Christ. Their presuppositions and prejudices,
their ignorance and confusion, have to be swept aside by
love and truth. In going out to make disciples we start off
with colossal hindrances in the way. Only with the
authority of Christ and the power of the Holy Spirit will
there be any breakthrough. Only as we are sensitive to
people, obedient to the Word of God and flexible within

the limits of the law of Christ, will we share in God's great
evangelistic purposes.

References
1. R.C.H. Lenski, *The Interpretation of St. Matthew's Gospel*,
   p. 1171.
2. Richard Eaxter, *The Reformed Pastor*, The Banner of Truth
   Trust, p. 184.
3. Frank Tillapaugh, *The Church Unleashed*, Regel Books, p. 5.
4. Jim Petersen, *Evangelism as a Lifestyle*, NavPress, p. 104.
5. *Ibid.* pp. 130, 136.
6. Genesis 18:18; Psalm 67; Isaiah 11:10; 42:1,6; 60:1–3; 66:19;
   cf. Matthew 4:13–17.
7. Matthew 5:14; 24:14; Mark 14:9; John 3:16–17; 12:46; Acts
   1:8
8. Acts 10:42; 2 Timothy 4:17; 1 Timothy 3:16; cf. Romans
   16:25–26, Colossians 1:23.

7

Being the 'friends of sinners'

Going out to make disciples does not begin with the giving out of a tract, extending an invitation to a 'gospel' meeting, or engaging in outdoor preaching. It is far more basic. The process of discipling begins at a much earlier stage and on a far broader scale! Ideally Christians are engaged in making disciples whenever and wherever they have contact with unbelievers! If we were able to see our whole 'life-style' (what the AV so aptly calls 'walk', see Ephesians 4:1) in the context of evangelism it would not only improve our approach to non-Christians but also provide a stimulus to greater holiness.

The prevalent view of evangelism centres concern on activity – doing things which are regarded as 'evangelistic,' through means of the written or spoken word. Generally these means of communication have a fairly limited content, referred to as 'the gospel', that is, something said about God's righteousness and holiness, a declaration of the sinfulness of human beings, a proclamation of the sufferings and death of Christ and a call to personal repentance and faith. Biblical evangelism, however, is not primarily focused upon what Christians *do* but upon what Christians *are*!

Whether we like the responsibility or not, we begin to be witnesses to the Lord Jesus Christ and his gospel from the moment of conversion. As soon as we profess faith in Christ our living testimony commences and we either commend or dishonour the gospel of Christ. The credibility of the gospel to a lost world is largely in the hands of the church. We bear the name of Christ. He will be judged to a large extent by our behaviour. When a Christian sticks a text in his car window he is 'nailing his colours to the mast' as it were. His driving had better be impeccable! Any driving infringements, lack of courtesy or ill temper will do more harm for the gospel than the good done by twenty texts! It is a sobering thought to know something of the responsibility which lies upon us. The world judges us before it judges our doctrine! The Holy Spirit has called us to *live* 'to the glory and praise of God' (Philippians 1:11).

The quality of Christian life

The apostle Paul urged the Ephesians: 'I . . . beseech you to have a walk worthy of the calling with which you were called' (Ephesians 4:1). They were called to belong to God, to be children of God, so let them live accordingly. They should therefore believe his teachings, trust his promises and obey his will. Paul is saying in effect, 'If you are believers, and wish to be known as believers, then live like believers!'

In earlier chapters we have emphasized the need for prayer. This was the pattern of the first Christians. Prayer was the first apostolic method in evangelism, consistency of life was the second. In the Acts of the Apostles both the Christian life and the Christian message are called 'the way'. Nine times the expression is used, so that an unmistakable emphasis is put upon the 'manner of life'. Christianity is not so much a set of doctrines but more 'a way of life'. Doctrine is of no value at all if it is not translated into practice in our daily living.

Before any specific plans are laid for evangelistic outreach, before any concern about the presentation of the gospel to the unconverted, the crucial question has to be faced by each believer: 'Is my life consistent with the gospel I profess?' Inconsistency not only hinders gospel presentation, but it can effectively destroy Christian credibility and thwart all future evangelism. The world will conclude, 'Christians are all hypocrites. They say one thing and do another. They profess with their lips and deny it with their lives!'

In the work of evangelism the single most important factor which influences the unconverted is the quality of the life we live. Our words will carry no weight if our behaviour is out of keeping with what we believe. That old adage, 'Practise what you preach!' is still of prime importance. Again there is truth in the saying: 'I cannot hear what you are saying because your life is making too much noise!' Inconsistency between words and works renders our message empty.

Where in the letters of the New Testament is the teaching about 'witnessing', in the sense of personal confrontation of the unsaved with the claims of Christ? The emphasis is placed upon our 'being'. For example: 'Only let your conduct be worthy of the gospel of Christ . . .' (Philippians 1:27). 'Aspire to lead a quiet life, to mind your own business, and to work with your own hands, as we commanded you, that you may walk properly towards those who are outside' (1 Thessalonians

4:11–12). 'See then that you walk circumspectly, not as fools but as wise' (Ephesians 5:15). Drawing the various strands together, we see that believers are expected to live properly, honestly, decently, with good outward appearance, upholding the standards which allegiance to Christ requires.

A life characterized by love

The greatest characteristic in the Christian life is love. It is the 'more excellent way' (1 Corinthians 12:31). Love for God and love for our neighbour are the hall marks of children of God as they seek to fulfil the law of the Lord (Matthew 22:37–39). A loving disposition towards brothers and sisters in Christ is a confirmation that one has passed from death to life (1 John 3:14). To love one another as Christ has loved us gives clear evidence that we are disciples of the Nazarene (John 13:34–35). There is an obligation of love laid upon us with regard to those outside of Christ too. Our Lord requires love, not just to those who love us but to those who are our enemies (Matthew 5:43–48). By this means demonstration is made of our sonship as we behave like our heavenly Father (Matthew 5:45).

God's love – the heart of the gospel

God the Father loved the world so much as to give his only begotten Son (John 3:16). 'He did not spare his own Son, but delivered him up for us all' (Romans 8:23). Jesus Christ loved his Father and his people so much as to become a human being and give himself up to the cross to deal with all our problems in one momentous event (Galatians 2:20; Ephesians 5:25–27).

Our love for God and for other human beings is not only 'the fulfilment of the law' (Romans 13:10); it is the only satisfactory response to God for his great love towards us. 'We love [God] because he first loved us' (1 John 4:19). When Paul wrote to the Ephesians he expressed his greatest desire for them: 'that Christ may dwell in your hearts through faith; that you, being rooted and grounded in love, may be able to comprehend with all the saints what is the width and length and depth and height – to know the love of Christ which passes knowledge; that you may be filled with all the fulness of God' (Ephesians 3:17–19).

'The love of God has been poured out in our hearts by the Holy Spirit who was given to us' (Romans 5:5). The first characteristic of the fruit of the Holy Spirit is love (Galatians 5:22). (Someone has said that love is the main characteristic from which all the rest are derived and to which they are subordinate.) However, it is relatively easy to place emphasis upon love in words, spoken or written, and quite a different matter to put the demands of love into practice. Here, as with everything else connected with our walk before God, the Lord Jesus Christ is our supreme example. He shows what love is all about. The cross is the demonstration of Christ's love to the Father (John 14:31), a love manifestly humble and obedient (Philippians 2:8). The cross is the revealing of Christ's love towards his people (John 15:13; 10:11; Galatians 2:20; Ephesians 5:25), a self-giving and self-sacrificing love.

My purpose, at this point, is to show how Christ demonstrated love to those yet unconverted. Simply telling people the good news is not following the example of Christ nor fulfilling our obligation to evangelize.

Love like Christ loves

We have the responsibility to try to love the unconverted
in the manner in which Christ loves them. While upon
earth our Saviour earned the reputation of being 'a friend
of sinners' (Matthew 11:19). Does the Christian church
today have such a reputation? Do outsiders, the lost,
bewildered and confused, know that we love them, and
that we are friendly? Do the self-righteous and those who
are 'respectably religious' hurl insults at us for our
association with the needy, desperate and hopeless
people of this world? The context of Matthew 11:19 is
very instructive. Our Lord has two sets of people in mind.
There are those who responded warmly to his teaching
and way of life. Such people found Jesus approachable.
On the other hand there were those with rigid religious
ideas who violently objected to his life-style and association with the outcast and hopeless.

Our Lord's reaction to these two classes of people is
clear and emphatic. To the downcast and crushed he
issued one of the most tender and gracious invitations
which could ever be expressed: 'Come to me, all you who
labour and are heavy laden and I will give you rest. Take
my yoke upon you and learn from me, for I am gentle and
lowly in heart, and you will find rest for your souls. For
my yoke is easy [lit., kind] and my burden is light'
(Matthew 11:28–30). Those Jews who were staggering
under an impossible burden (Acts 15:10), those who were
struggling to please God but failing abysmally, those who
had fallen under the law of Sinai and saw no way back to
God open to them – such people were being invited to
turn to Christ and take his 'kind' yoke upon them.
Helpless and lost sinners were being offered a way of
hope. Weak sinners were being offered support and
strength to see them through. Our Lord was inviting the

spiritually broken, weak and sickly to be unequally yoked to him! The believer is harnessed into the yoke with Christ and it is Christ who does all the hard work. Indeed, to follow the analogy right through, it is Christ who shoulders all the burden and carries the believer as well! Christ's yoke is 'kind' because instead of imposing pressure to weigh down it communicates strength and help to carry all burdens. Yoked up with him, 'I can do all things through Christ who strengthens me' (Philippians 4:13).

By stark contrast the Pharisees, and other Jews like them, reacted viciously to the teaching and behaviour of our Saviour. They were the 'respectable', self-righteous, 'religious' types whose hearts knew no living experience of the true God. To these people Christ had only words of rebuke and condemnation (Matthew 11:20–24). The law of Moses was intended as a 'disciplinarian', to restrict and hedge in the people of God and prepare them to welcome Christ gladly, that they might receive that righteousness which comes by faith in him (Galatians 2:21; 3:24). The scribes and Pharisees treated the law as a means of self-justification, as a ladder to climb by their own efforts into the acceptable presence of God. We know there is only one ladder, the one prefigured in Jacob's ladder of old, and that is the Lord Jesus Christ (Genesis 28:12; cf. John 1:51).

To those who were godly the law was to be understood as the means of exposing their sinfulness (Romans 3:20), of humbling them and causing them to long for better days – like the promised time of the New Covenant when God would give them a new heart and put his spirit within them (Ezekiel 36:26), place his law in their minds and write it on their hearts (Jeremiah 31:33).

The Lord shows love to the penitent woman

The contrast between the Pharisees and outcast sinners

came into sharp prominence immediately following our Lord's gracious invitation in Matthew 11:28–30 (cf. Matthew 11:1–19; Luke 7:18–35. Both Boettner and Fuller place Luke 7:36–50 immediately after Matthew 11:30).

Simon the Pharisee invited our Lord to his home for a meal. The Saviour willingly accepted. Indeed it was clearly his practice to respond favourably to any such invitations (Luke 7:36; 11:37; 14:1). It is sometimes the spontaneous response of a new convert to want to invite new Christian friends home for tea (Luke 5:29). What a natural way to deepen the bonds of fellowship and also to meet with more unbelievers on what might be termed 'neutral territory'! Sad to say, many Christians appear awkward and uncomfortable with the unsaved and do not know how to make 'ordinary' conversation. We should not feel under compulsion to force every occasion into a gospel encounter. The unsaved may find it a refreshing surprise that we can hold intelligent conversation on other matters besides 'religion'! While an invitation to a meal may be the loving response of the newly converted it may also be an opportunity for a sincere enquirer to learn more of the Christian way. However, there is no guarantee that it will not be used by enemies who are lying in wait to trap us in our talk and behaviour, or by those who are nothing less than cold-hearted, inquisitive folk!

Our Lord accepted Simon's invitation though the latter's motive was far from clear. Into Simon's home walked 'a woman . . . who was a sinner' (Luke 7:37). Unannounced, uninvited and clearly unwelcome by the host, she brought a gift for Jesus. This is one of the most beautiful incidents recorded in the Scriptures. It is designed to bring before our eyes the Lord of glory in all his wisdom and love as he receives a sinner and yet at the same time puts a self-righteous Pharisee to shame.

She was a sinner

This woman had become a great sinner in her own eyes, and this was the real difference between her and the Pharisee. She had listened to Jesus as he taught the people. Maybe she had heard the actual words of the gracious invitation (Matthew 11:28–30), or at least something very closely allied to it. She had been brought so low. Helpless and lost, she suddenly saw a way of hope opened to her. In that deep grief which comes through repentance, yet at the same time with a sense of wonder and gratitude at her acceptance by the Lord Jesus Christ, she came to be near him. Her responding love sought the assurance of the Saviour's love. See how repenting sinners have generally a twofold agony to endure: they have to bear the mockery, criticism and scorn of their former friends and associates, and also the proud contempt of the virtuous and pious! The second is the hardest to bear. But the love of Christ constrained her. Love for the Saviour drew her even to the Pharisee's house, even to endure abuse from so proud and pious a man!

The problem

A big problem facing Christians as they seek to be friendly towards sinners is not the unbelievers outside the church, but professing Christians inside the church. Whenever Christians try to follow Christ in reaching out to the needy and lost they will run the risk of offending a considerable number of folk within the churches. Pharisees are still with us! The Lord Jesus faced a generation hard to please (Matthew 11:16–19). The Lord had done everything to stir the heart of the unbeliever.

J.C. Ryle identified the problem clearly: 'The Jews, in

our Lord's time, found fault with every teacher whom God sent among them. First came John the Baptist, preaching repentance: an austere man, a man who withdrew himself from society, and lived an ascetic life. Did this satisfy the Jews? No! They found fault and said, "He hath a devil." Then came Jesus the Son of God, preaching the Gospel: living as other men lived, and practising none of John the Baptist's peculiar austerities. And did this satisfy the Jews? No! They found fault again, and said, "Behold a man gluttonous and a wine-bibber, a friend of publicans and sinners." In short, they were as perverse and hard to please as wayward children. It is a mournful fact, that there are always thousands of professing Christians just as unreasonable as these Jews. They are equally perverse, and equally hard to please: whatever we teach and preach, they find fault; whatever be our manner of life, they are dissatisfied![1]

The challenge

The challenge facing the church today is 'Do we have the reputation which our Lord had while here on earth?' Do we have the name for being the friends of sinners? Christ had a profound interest and concern for those who were generally avoided or ignored. Look at his tenderness and understanding with the deaf and dumb, the blind, the leper, the epileptic, the lame, the bereaved, the bewildered and the mentally disturbed. He loved people and it showed! He visited their homes. He was approachable by all and sundry. He went to the homes of people who had bad reputations – Zacchaeus and Matthew Levi, the son of Alphaeus. He mixed with their friends. He made wine, good quality wine, for an embarrassed host at a wedding. Seeing the deeper significance of the water for Jewish purification being changed into best quality wine does not lessen the act itself!

Jesus had compassion on people and it was blatantly obvious. He loved those who were hurting and in great need. Love moved him to preach 'the gospel of the kingdom' and heal 'every sickness and every disease among the people . . . He was moved with compassion for them, because they were weary and scattered, like sheep having no shepherd' (Matthew 9:35–36).

Does the world have such a view of the Christian church today? The staggering number of people with broken marriages, the phenomenal number of people with mental disorders and emotional disturbances of one sort and another, the unemployed with acute feelings of rejection and uselessness – where do all these people turn? Do they ever turn to Christians? Have we the reputation of friendliness and concern? Are Christians today approachable or aloof?

A further dilemma – friendship with the world

A further problem faces the people of God. How do we reconcile this friendship for sinners with that friendship which is incompatible with love for God? James writes, 'Do you not know that friendship with the world is enmity with God?'(James 4:4.) 'The world' and 'God' are to be seen as being diametrically opposed. Friendship with one means hostility towards the other; to love one means to hate the other. In the letter of James, as in the letter of the apostle John, the issue at stake is that the people of God must not try to love two opposing objects: God and the world. To love the Lord and love the world is to commit spiritual adultery. It is clear from the letter of James that some of those referred to as 'brethren'

(James 1:2) were guilty of this form of adultery (James 4:4).

Rudolf Stier explains this usage of the word 'adultery': 'A hard word of guilt and shame, even if it referred only to those sins of the flesh which the words ordinarily denote – the breaking of the bond of marriage among men. Although even in our own day there may be much more secret adultery manifest to God in Christian communities than is generally thought – what man would be able to endure the public rebuke of being an adulterer, and what woman that of being an adulteress? But that is but a slight thing in comparison of the sin which St James means. He uses the word in the same sense as that in which the Prophets used it, when they condemned Israel's apostasy; as that in which the Lord Jesus used it, when He rebuked the wicked and adulterous spirit of His generation (Matthew 12:39), and when again, with reference to the future of His people, He spoke of an adulterous and sinful generation before which no disciple must be ashamed of Him and His words, who would not that the returning Son of man should be ashamed of him (Mark 8:38). An evil race are all men by nature; but wicked and adulterous those only can be called who belong to the people of God, and yet live carnally and after the course of the world.'[2]

It is evident that James is concerned about love for the world, not in the sense of loving sinners with a view to their conversion, but rather in the sense of being like them. When believers are motivated by a desire for the approval and appreciation of unconverted people and seek to live just as they live, then they show they are in love with the world. The apostle John expands the thought: 'Do not love the world or the things in the world. If anyone loves the world, the love of the Father is not in him. For all that is in the world – the lust of the flesh, the lust of the eyes, and the pride of life – is not of the Father but is of the world' (1 John 2:15–16). Once we 'were dead in trespasses and sins' and living 'according to the course of this world' (Ephesians 2:1–2), but from conversion we are to 'put off' this old way of life and 'put on' the new, 'which was created according to God, in righteousness and true holiness' (Ephesians 4:22,24).

The godly man does not turn to the worldly and unconverted for advice, nor does he mix with them in order to identify with them in their behaviour, nor yet join in with their bad conversations (Psalm 1:1). Friendship with those who are of the world is always on our terms, not theirs. It may sound trite to speak of being '*in* the world without being *of* it', but this effectively describes our Lord's own sentiment in his high priestly prayer: 'I do not pray that you should take them out of the world, but that you should keep them from the evil' (John 17:14). Learning to live amongst corruption without being contaminated is the true secret of holiness. Our Saviour freely mixed with sinners and yet was perfectly 'holy, harmless, undefiled, separate from sinners' (Hebrews 7:26). There is no alternative open to us. Holiness is not to be achieved in the isolation and seclusion of a monastery. Rather it is to be achieved under pressure within a hostile environment. Biblical evangelism is not accomplished by an occasional foray into the world. We are in the world. This is where our Lord wants us to be. Work has to be done while it is day (John 9:4). The time for rest comes later! (Revelation 14:13.)

Reference
1. J.C. Ryle, *Matthew's Gospel*, James Clarke, p. 112.
2. Rudolf Stier, *Commentary on James*, James Family Christian Publishing Co., p. 408.

— 8 —

Gospel flexibility

The approach of the Christian church to the unsaved has often been highly stereotyped. We need to grapple with the great principles of evangelism outlined in the Scriptures. One such principle is that propounded so forcefully by the apostle Paul in writing to the Corinthians: 'For though I am free from all men, I have made myself a servant to all, that I might win the more; and to the Jews I became as a Jew, that I might win Jews; to those who are under the law, as under the law, that I might win those who are under the law; to those who are without law, as without law (not being without law towards God, but under law towards Christ), that I might win those who are without law; to the weak I became as weak, that I might win the weak. I have become all things to all men, that I might by all means save some. Now this I do for the gospel's sake . . .' (1 Corinthians 9:19–23). Being a Christian, as distinct from being a Jew, Paul was aware of a new freedom under the gospel of Christ. It is a very wonderful experience to know 'the liberty by which Christ has made us free' (Galatians 5:1).

The distinguishing features between the new covenant and the old are considerable. Some main differences need to be brought out to establish the approach required of believers towards unbelievers under the conditions of the new covenant.

The old and new covenants

Under the old covenant salvation depended upon integration into the nation of Israel. God's gracious working was localized in that small, insignificant race. The Israelites were often affectionately designated by God as 'my people' (eg. Exodus 7:16; Isaiah 40:1; 51:4). Others who were to experience the Lord's favour were brought in and identified with them. The notable example of Rahab the prostitute serves to illustrate the point. At the fall of Jericho Rahab was delivered from death and accepted because of her 'faith working through love' (Galatians 5:6; cf. James 2:25–26). She was then incorporated into the nation of Israel (Matthew 1:5) and thereby shared the privileges of those who received 'the adoption, the glory, the covenants, the giving of the law, the service of God, and the promises' (Romans 9:4–5).

A further striking example of this total identity with Israel is that of the Gentile Ruth. Naomi, her mother-in-law, had given instruction to her two daughters-in-law that they should return to their own people, the Moabites. Orpah kissed Naomi and returned to her kin. Ruth clung to Naomi and pleaded with her that she might stay:

'Entreat me not to leave you,
    or to turn back from following after you;
for wherever you go, I will go;

and wherever you lodge, I will lodge;
your people shall be my people,
and your God, my God' (Ruth 1:16).

Ruth, like Rahab, was established into the royal line, that is, the genealogy of Christ (Matthew 1:5).

Israel of old was a theocratic nation in which moral, ceremonial and civil law were integrated in one united whole. There were clear detailed laws governing each area of life. God gave meticulous instructions to distinguish Israel from the rest of the nations. Under the new covenant the situation is drastically altered. The people of God are now to be found among all the various nations. Children of God are, by God's design, to be called out from 'every tribe and tongue and people and nation' of the earth (Revelation 5:9), not into a physical race with a single geographic location but into a spiritual race which remains physically scattered among the nations. Among his own kith and kin the new covenant believer is to exercise his influence (1 Peter 2:9–10).

Along with the change of emphasis from the national Israel to the spiritual Israel, now spread throughout the world, have come vital changes in religious and civil requirements. Blood sacrifices are now at an end because of the great sacrifice of the Lord Jesus Christ (Hebrews 10:1–10). The temple of Jerusalem no longer has significance because the true temple has come, which is Christ and those who are 'in' him (John 2:19–22: 1 Corinthians 6:19–20; 1 Peter 2:4–5). The old Levitical priesthood is ended because the King-Priest after the order of Melchizedek, Jesus Christ, God's own Son, is now our High Priest (Hebrews 7:1–19; cf. 1:5). Great and lasting are the changes brought about by the advent of Jesus Christ and the outpouring of the Holy Spirit. The key of the new covenant is the spiritual fulfilment of old covenant types and shadows (Colossians 2:13–17). The glorious realization of 'the mystery of God's will' (Ephesians 1:9) is found in Christ and in his church from all races, which is scattered among the nations (Colossians 1:26–27).

Gospel liberty

Under the new covenant a liberty is granted to believers which a Jew under the old covenant would never have dreamed possible: 'All things are lawful for me, but all things are not helpful. All things are lawful for me, but I will not be brought under the power of any' (1 Corinthians 6:12). 'All things are lawful for me, but all things are not helpful; all things are lawful for me, but all things do not edify' (1 Corinthians 10:23).

Of course, we cannot take these verses out of the context of Scripture as a whole. The 'all things' are certainly qualified by so much which is required in other places. All things are lawful for the Christian, when in themselves neither commanded nor forbidden under the terms of the new covenant, set out clearly in Scripture. However, though the New Testament believer experiences a much greater liberty and freedom than anything ever known by a godly Jew, we have a much greater responsibility imposed upon us. Even when something is 'lawful' it may not be expedient. All Christians are expected to learn to think clearly and carefully and 'walk circumspectly, not as fools but as wise' (Ephesians 5:15).

Walter Craddock makes useful observations: 'If you look to the rule of expediency you will walk a hundred times stricter, than men that only look what is lawful, and what is not ... All things, in all places, at all times, and in all circumstances, are not expedient for all persons ...

There are abundance of things that are lawful, that do not honour God, that do not win sinners, and build up saints.'[1] Walter Craddock establishes four simple guidelines in order to determine what is expedient:

1. Will it glorify God?
2. Will it build up my brethren?
3. Will it be profitable to those outside?
4. Will it benefit my own soul?

Judging by these criteria Christians may arrive at different conclusions depending upon the circumstances. Such flexibility strikes horror into the heart of many Christians! They prefer the easier course of legalism where the rules are laid out in detail. When all is said and done a legalist does not have to think!

Gospel flexibility

Gospel liberty is a distinct New Testament blessing. As it relates to evangelism it presents the Christian with flexibility to adjust to those he is seeking to win.

The evangelistic principle, 'all things to all men, that I might by all means save some' (1 Corinthians 9:22), is not a formula to allow any practice or approach which 'might' save someone! This text has been used to justify the most outlandish and the most childish evangelistic efforts. Rather it is a clear principle of the new covenant by which Christians can make themselves approachable and 'friendly'! It is not a question of compromise, but rather adaptability within the restrictions imposed by the law of Christ.

Walter Craddock poses another question: 'How could [Paul] comply thus to win and save souls, unless there

were a latitude given by Christ, wherein there is a liberty
that is not determined, and the saints may apply themselves to, for the glory of God and the good of others? . . .
He could be a weak professor with the weak, and strong
with the strong, and be circumcised, and shave his head;
and when he was among the Gentiles he could show his
freedom, and win them; he could be all things to all men,
which he could not have been, if there had not been a
latitude in the Gospel, that people may use to the glory of
God, and the good of others.'[2]

The law of Christ

In order to combat the possible charge of antinomianism
(being without law) the apostle Paul indicated his constant commitment to the commandments of the Lord –
not in the old covenant sense as defined in the law of
Moses but in the new covenant sense as 'married' to
Christ (Romans 7:1–6) and therefore under the obligation
of love to him, not only in behaviour (2 Corinthians 5:14),
but also in thinking (2 Corinthians 10:5).

Jim Petersen pleads for flexibility in our approach to
the unsaved: 'It is our responsibility to adapt to them
unless absolute moral issues are involved. Make them feel
comfortable around you. Be "all things to all men".
Remember that sanctification is a matter of the heart, not
surroundings.'[3] The aim is to share our faith naturally
and in a relaxed manner. Flexibility is not the same as
compromise. We are to exercise our God-given faculties
and think through our approach in each new situation. In
reaching out to the unsaved there are two extremes to
which believers often resort. One is to identify with them
to such an extent that there is a sinful conformity
(Romans 12:2). The other is to keep non-Christians at a

'safe' distance. An invisible gulf is fixed between 'us' and 'them'. Invitations are extended across the gap. Reassurances are given of a welcome if they come over but no real personal contact takes place. God-honouring evangelism requires a warm expression of friendship. People must be made to feel that they matter. Knowing that all human beings are created in the image of God (Genesis 1:27) necessitates our treating others with dignity and respect. 'What you have to do is to take time with him, to make friends with him, to get alongside him, to find out where he is in terms of spiritual understanding, and to start dealing with him at that point. You have to explain the gospel to him, and be sure that he understands it and is convinced of its truth, before you start pressing him to an active response.'[4]

Inconsistency

Paul's attitude with regard to the circumcisions of Timothy and Titus left the apostle open to the charge of inconsistency. Timothy was circumcised 'because of the Jews' (Acts 16:1–5). Titus was not circumcised – even though considerable pressure was brought upon him by 'false brethren' (Galatians 2:3–5). Charles Hodge writes, 'The former he circumcised, because it was regarded as a concession. The latter he refused to circumcise, because it was demanded as a matter of necessity.'[5] It is impossible for the Christian to be consistent in outward behaviour in every instance. Each situation must be judged upon its own merits. Discerning the areas where flexibility is not only possible, but required of us for the saving of souls, is no easy matter. Clearly a good working knowledge of the Scriptures coupled with godliness and spiritual maturity are essential prerequisites for discernment (Hebrews

5:12–14). To quote Charles Hodge again, 'No one was more yielding in matters of indifference, no one was more unyielding in matters of principle than this apostle. So long as things indifferent were regarded as such, he was ready to accommodate himself to the most unreasonable prejudices; but when they were insisted upon as matters of necessity, he would not give place, no not for an hour, Galatians 2:5.'[6]

There is not only the problem of discerning when an issue is open to a flexible approach and when there is no latitude whatsoever; there is also the difficulty of understanding the people themselves. When are they 'weak' and when are they just plain 'awkward'? John Calvin warned of this dilemma: 'We must adapt ourselves to the weak, but not to the stubborn. [Paul's] purpose was to bring them to Christ, not to further his own interests, or to retain their goodwill.'[7]

Yet are we really expected to go as far as Fredrick Godet would have us believe? He writes of Paul: 'No observance appeared to him too irksome, no requirement too stupid, no prejudice too absurd, to prevent his dealing tenderly with it in the view of saving souls.'[8] The key is 'his dealing tenderly with it in the view of saving souls', or, in the words of Paul, 'Now this I do for the gospel's sake' (1 Corinthians 9:23).

It is not only believers, but also many of the unsaved in our society, who want a rigid approach from us. We shall not lack critics, either inside or outside the church, when we attempt a flexible approach in evangelism. All we can hope to do is to live the life of a Christian, clearly and blatantly before the world, to be flexible, approachable, friendly, adaptable, immovable where the law of Christ is concerned or when the honour of the gospel is endangered, but on all other matters to show a remarkable amiability. 'The gospel . . . is the power of God to salvation for everyone who believes' (Romans 1:16). We cannot make the gospel acceptable to the unbelieving mind but we can obey God in our flexible approach towards the unsaved.

This flexibility may cause concern to the legalists among us. For too long we have been looking over our shoulder to ensure that our Christian brethren approved of our attitudes and practices. God's 'Word is truth' (John 17:17). It is 'a lamp to my feet and a light to my path' (Psalm 119:105). Our prayer should be that of the psalmist: 'Deal bountifully with your servant, that I may live and keep your word' (Psalm 119:17). We must not be bound by legalistic brethren when Christ has made us free!

The great gap

A most powerful discrimination is being exercised by concentrating evangelistic work on our buildings and limiting it to public preaching. Iain Murray wrote, 'The exercise of spiritual gifts by preaching elders in the meetings of the church is not the primary means by which the gospel spreads.'[9] Thousands of our fellow-citizens know virtually nothing about Christianity. Their concept of God is sentimental or pagan. Their understanding of the person and work of Christ, right-eousness, holiness, sin and salvation is virtually non-existent. Rarely, if ever, do thoughts concerning the true and living God enter their thinking. They behave as though God did not exist! In order to reach them a great gulf has to be spanned.

The chasm which divides us from the unbelieving world is colossal. We have to overcome a language barrier: they do not understand our biblical terms and concepts. We

are also confronted with a cultural barrier. The church has
been aware of the cultural differences between the races,
though whether we have effectively faced the issues involved is open to question. There is, however, an equally
serious, if not more serious, cultural gap within society as
a whole. Even within our own race and people there are
strong subcultures. There is a youth subculture, a 'pop'
subculture, a drug subculture . . . There are subcultures
related to geographic areas in Britain. Whether we can use
the old terms 'working class' and 'middle class' is to be
doubted. Social mobility has eradicated the old distinc-
tives. But subcultures nevertheless exist, though they are
much more difficult to define and evaluate. Can we face up
to the realization that true Christianity is a subculture?
The old values of our nation have almost gone. Post-
Christian culture has swept in with the force of a tornado.
Christian values no longer influence and direct the
'formal' or 'public' morals of the nation.

The church is clearly in a minority position. Of course,
true Christians have always been a remnant within our
nation, but many were beguiled into thinking otherwise
because of the considerable influence which the gospel
once exerted upon national life. The vestiges of
Christianity in the sense of language and outlook make it
harder to reach our countrymen who confuse church-going
with Christianity! We are going to meet terrific problems
when we try to cross the ravine from our subculture to the
rest of the community. Immense obstacles lie in our path
when we attempt to bring the gospel to those who do not
share our presuppositions, and who have not been
previously prepared to respond to a proclamation of the
gospel. Jim Petersen is right when he says, 'We are not
doing well in crossing these cultural frontiers. We are, in
fact, talking to ourselves!'[10]

A pagan society – lost and bewildered

In spite of the godlessness of our society, there are still people who are crying out for help. The breakdown of relationships, the escalation of the divorce rate, the disillusionment as family life no longer provides emotional stability and fulfilment, the rise in alcoholism and drug abuse, promiscuity, homosexuality and lesbianism – all conspire to leave people empty, dirty and without hope. Yet this is a tremendous opportunity for the gospel. At work, in the community, among relatives and friends, the Christian has a thousand opportunities to show the reality of Christian experience.

Some of the barriers which exist between the unsaved and the church are of our own making. The mystique of church life has been perpetuated. The reality of a life centring in Christ which is exciting, stimulating and satisfying has not been clearly presented. For those who are of the world Christianity is seen as either irrelevant worship in elaborately constructed and distinctly old-fashioned buildings, or as 'sin, damnation and hell-fire'! Men and women who are hopelessly lost have not been confronted with a vibrant Christian alternative.

The darker the world, the brighter the light shines. The apostle Paul urges Christians to keep this thought in mind: 'Do all things without murmuring and disputing, that you may become blameless and harmless, children of God without fault in the midst of a crooked and perverse generation, among whom you shine as lights in the world, holding fast the word of life . . .' (Philippians 2:14–15). The Lord influences the lives of his people. It is the Lord who determines where the light will shine and to what purpose. Our task is to obey his truth and seek grace and courage to be faithful to Christ and his gospel 'in this adulterous and sinful generation' (Mark 8:38).

Getting to know sinners

We have to learn to understand the world in which we
live. We have to keep abreast of the times. In each
generation and society the church needs those who will
follow in the steps of 'the children of Issachar who had
understanding of the times, to know what Israel ought to
do' (1 Chronicles 12:32). We may be thankful that there
are those in our own day who have the ability to evaluate
and challenge the world on its own ground. The vast
majority of Christians do not need to take a degree in
sociology to know what is going on around them. Two
things should be studied with care and persistence –
Scripture and people! Get to know people and relate what
you learn to the teachings of Scripture. The Bible is the
finest book on sociology, psychology, anthropology, etc.
Studying the Bible and getting to know people takes time.
This is probably the hardest part of all. Behind Paul's
flexible approach to people for the sake of the gospel
there is something taken for granted which can soon be
verified by a glance at the Acts and his thirteen letters –
he spent a lot of time with people! Much of his work
related to the calling he had received as an evangelist and
to the fact that he was supported on occasions by the
churches (Philippians 4:15–16). However, those who are
not called to be evangelists need seriously to ask whether
they are spending enough time with the unsaved!

Prosperity or people?

Building good relationships with people involves time
and effort. Most Christians are incredibly busy people.
For this reason it may be appropriate to ask whether a
radical adjustment of commitments is necessary.

Christian men, by and large, spend far too much time and effort on their careers. Whether for financial gains or the fulfilment of personal ambition, so many project the impression that they live to work rather than work to live. Amassing treasure on earth is a futile occupation (Matthew 6:19–21). Why should it be thought that promotion and increased work responsibility is always a gift from the Lord? Too often it is a device of Satan to draw men away from their useful service in the church of Christ. Christian wives and mothers are not free from the allurement of paid employment. Whether motivated by a desire for the 'little extras' or to maintain a standard of living which their husbands' income will not allow, or to get out of the house and find fulfilment in work which is financially remunerated, our sisters are incredibly over-worked. Furthermore, fit, active and capable sisters are no longer available for the many responsibilities which God requires of them in the church and in the community at large. Opportunities for love and care exist on every hand. Godly women with intelligence, charity and zeal could do so much for the glory of God (1 Timothy 5:9).

People matter more than things! Christian men may leave a large bank balance for their wives and children; they may leave a successful business to their successor; they may have made an impact on their profession or trade – but it will all decay. 'For we brought nothing into this world, and it is certain that we can carry nothing out. And having food and clothing, with these we shall be content' (1 Timothy 6:7–8).

How much better to use our time for people! Make friends here and now with a view to having friends for eternity! John Wesley once said, 'No man ever went to heaven alone; he must either find friends or make them.' The things of this world are passing. How good it will be to be welcomed by brethren and sisters in heaven, those

who will thank God for our friendship to them when they
were without hope and without God in the world!

Evangelism is 90% love

It is said that 90% of evangelism is love. We are to love
people as they are and as individuals, not as targets for
evangelism. Love, accept, adapt, be a friend. The apostle
Paul revealed his own attitude towards the Thessalonians:
'So, affectionately longing for you, we were well pleased to
impart to you not only the gospel of God, but also our own
lives, because you had become dear to us' (1 Thessalonians
2:8). A genuine friendliness is the prime mark of the man
who is learning to love his neighbour as himself. God
willing, we shall love them into the kingdom of Christ!

References
 1. Walter Craddock, *Gospel Liberty*, p. 7. Printed along with
    other sermons under the general heading of *Gospel Holiness*,
    Thomas ~rewsters of London, 1655.
 2. *Ibid* p. 12.
 3. Jim Petersen, *Evangelism as a Lifestyle*, NavPress, p. 139.
 4. J.I. Packer, *Evangelism and the Sovereignty of God*, IVP, p. 120.
 5. Charles Hodge, *Commentary on First Corinthians*, Banner of
    Truth Trust, p. 164.
 6. *Ibid*, p. 163.
 7. John Calvin, *Commentary on First Corinthians*, Saint Andrew
    Press, p. 196.
 8. Fredrick L. Godet, *Commentary on First Corinthians*, Kregel
    Publications, p. 468.
 9. *Banner of Truth* Magazine, February 1977, p. 21, quoted by R.
    Joslin, *Urban Harvest*, Evangelical Press, p. 97.
10. Jim Petersen, *Evangelism as a Lifestyle*, p. 20.

— 9 —

Ready to give a reason!

Biblical evangelism is perilous! God requires his people to be involved in the world. We are to be 'the light of the world' (Matthew 5:14). Fulfilling this commission requires that we make an impact upon the society in which we live. The church of Jesus Christ is no secret club operating behind locked doors. The confident assertion of the apostle Paul before King Agrippa is the believer's constant boast: 'This thing was not done in a corner' (Acts 26:26). We are 'not ashamed of the gospel of Christ, for it is the power of God to salvation for everyone who believes' (Romans 1:16). We are 'children of light' (Ephesians 5:8). 'He who does the truth comes to the light, that his deeds may be clearly seen, that they have been done in God' (John 3:21).

The pressure upon the believer 'in this adulterous and sinful generation' (Mark 8:38) is never to be under-estimated. Only the intercession of our Lord and the power of our God will keep us safe in such an alien environment (John 17:15; 1 Peter 1:5). There is a great

temptation to 'opt out' and purchase a small cottage in a
desolate part of Britain with just enough land to grow
sufficient food and raise a few hens and sheep! Such an
escape is not to be. Nor are we to resort to the 'holy huddle'
in a spiritual ghetto involved only with believers. The
lighthouse must be in the most effective location. Its light
warns of the destructive rocks and indicates the safe way
home. Well did Paul urge the Philippians to unity and holy
living in the church: 'Do all things without murmuring and
disputing, that you may become blameless and harmless,
children of God without fault in the midst of a crooked and
perverse generation, among whom you shine as lights in
the world, holding fast the word of life' (Philippians
2:14–16). All through the early chapters of his first letter
the apostle Peter shows his awareness of the fact that those
who devote themselves to the service of the living and true
God would be open to gross misunderstanding, ill-will,
hatred and violence. So he writes, 'Even if you should
suffer for righteousness' sake, you are blessed' (1 Peter
3:14). Confronted with the sinfulness and hostility of the
world the Christian is not to be afraid. Peter quotes Isaiah
8:12–14:

'Do not . . . be afraid of their threats, nor be troubled.
The Lord of hosts, him you shall hallow;
let him be your fear,
and let him be your dread.
He will be as a sanctuary . . .'

It is like the teaching of the Lord Jesus Christ: 'And I say
to you, my friends, do not be afraid of those who kill the
body, and after that have no more that they can do. But I
will show you whom you should fear: fear him who, after
he has killed, has power to cast into hell; yes, I say to you,
fear him!' (Luke 12:4–5.)

Reaching out to the unsaved is time-consuming and dangerous. However, with God's presence by his Spirit, it can be a most exciting adventure. Love for our neighbour means a desire to see him come out of darkness into light. Darkness must not be allowed to overcome the light!

Involvement does not mean contamination

The Lord Jesus is the example of holy living in an unholy world. The Bible is clear and emphatic about the character of the Lord. He had no inherent sin. He was as 'a lamb without blemish and without spot' (1 Peter 1:19). He was 'holy, harmless, undefiled, separate from sinners' (Hebrews 7:26). We can say that Christ was 'made sin' (2 Corinthians 5:21), but we cannot say that he was made sinful. We can say that God sent 'his own Son *in the likeness of* sinful flesh' (Romans 8:3), but not *in* sinful flesh'.

Believers start out at a different point. We are born sinners – now saved by the grace of God. Like the Christians at Corinth we are 'sanctified in Christ Jesus, called to be saints' (1 Corinthians 1:2). Holy living in an unholy world is only possible for us as we abide in Christ and obey him. He is able to create a spiritual cocoon around his people to protect them from contamination. This thought is often expressed in the Old Testament. In Psalm 18 King David has enemies in mind who are bent on his physical destruction. He would be the first to admit his even greater need for protection from spiritual destruction. So his words carry a double meaning:

'I will love you, O Lord, my strength.
The Lord is my rock and my fortress and my deliverer;
my God, my strength, in whom I will trust;

        my shield and the horn of my salvation, my
        stronghold' (Psalm 18:1–2).

The apostle Peter sets out three steps to be taken if we
are to be true to our holy calling and faithful in the
discharge of our responsibility to unbelievers: 'Sanctify
the Lord God in your hearts, and always be ready to give a
defence to everyone who asks you a reason for the hope
that is in you, with meekness and fear' (1 Peter 3:15).

1. 'Sanctify the Lord God in your hearts!'

The apostle Peter is concerned for the good name of the
gospel. In this first letter he gives sound practical advice
to all wives and husbands (1 Peter 3:1–7). He teaches a
godly wife how to live before her ungodly husband. He
teaches the godly husband how to treat his wife with
understanding, gentleness, respect and consideration. He
teaches the church how to live together with compassion,
love and courtesy. What an attractive way of living! Yet
sadly this is not the picture evident in many Christian
homes or churches in these days!

God's rule in the heart
To sanctify the Lord in the heart is to allow God to be the
centre of our whole existence. It is to desire his rule over
every area and department of life. The Lord Jesus was
asked by the Pharisees when the kingdom of God would
come. He answered them and said, 'The kingdom of God
does not come with observation; nor will they say, "See
here!" or "See there!" For indeed, the kingdom of God is
within you' (Luke 17:20–21). God's will and God's glory
are to be our chief goal. God-honouring evangelism can
only flow from those who love God and are devoted to

him. The Lord God is not only upon the throne in the centre of the whole created order (Revelation 4:2–3), ruling and working 'all things according to the counsel of his will' (Ephesians 1:11), he is also to reign in the hearts and lives of his people (Romans 5:21). The believer makes no contribution whatsoever to God's rule over his created order. God is the Sovereign Lord (Acts 4:24). Yet with respect to his rule in our hearts we have a great contribution to make. We yield to him, are subject to him in love and always ready to do his bidding, seeking his approval alone. The greatest motivation to obedience and love is a longing to please the heavenly Father! To receive his recognition and praise and hear him one day say, 'Well done, good and faithful servant . . . enter into the joy of your Lord' (Matthew 25:21), that is the real incentive to holiness and obedience! The secret is to live a 'Christ-centred' life, to have a daily awareness that we 'were dead in trespasses and sins' (Ephesians 2:1), and yet are now sinners saved by the grace of God (Ephesians 2:5,8). John Miller draws the following conclusion: 'As I experience the gospel as a message of God's total forgiveness, and Christ as the magnetic, personal centre of my life, evangelizing with a gospel of forgiveness is a natural and inevitable outgrowth.'[1] The Lord is our Protector and our Deliverer. We are to hold in our hearts an unwavering reliance upon his presence and his love and to honour him whether by life or death (Romans 14:8). Like godly Moses and Stephen we shall be able to endure 'as seeing him who is invisible' (Hebrews 11:27).

Sanctifying the Lord in the heart and walking in wisdom towards those who are outside are in reality two sides of one coin. As with Paul's words to the Romans in chapter 12, presenting our bodies a living sacrifice is one side; not being conformed to this world is the other. Our chief desire is to 'prove what is that good and acceptable and perfect will of God' (Romans 12:2), by the life we live and the answers we give. In other words, 'Aspire to lead a quiet life, to mind your own business, and to work with your own hands . . . that you may walk properly towards those who are outside, and that you may lack nothing' (1 Thessalonians 4:11–12). Lenski comments: 'This thing that God wills is the condition of the Thessalonians in which they are set wholly apart for God and are separated in life and conduct from the world which is not thus set apart and does not even know God.'[2]

To sanctify the Lord in the heart and to be sanctified by the Lord God (1 Peter 1:2) have essentially the same effect. Sanctification comes by the working of the Holy Spirit in the heart (Romans 15:16). The Holy Spirit applies the merit of Christ's blood (Hebrews 13:12) by which we are truly set apart for God's exclusive use. An important part of our sanctification comes by means of the Word of God (Ephesians 5:26). Godly living in a dirty and wicked world can only be achieved in God's way. The conflict between separation and involvement in the world is only achieved through a careful reading, study and application of the Scriptures. As Jesus prayed, 'Sanctify them by your truth. Your word is truth' (John 17:17).

2. 'Always ready' to give an explanation

Opportunities will arise without force and without strain for reference to be made to one's personal commitment. The approach of 'always being ready to give an explanation' avoids the extremes of an unholy forcefulness on the one hand and a total silence on the other. One of the terms bandied about in Christian circles is 'aggressive evangelism'. This smacks too much of the salesman who will insist on putting his foot in the door and keeping you talking until, worn out by his sheer persistence, you yield and purchase his product! Jim Packer gets right to the point: 'Indiscriminate buttonholing, the intrusive barging in to the privacy of other people's souls, the thick-skinned insistence on expounding the things of God to reluctant strangers who are longing to get away – these modes of behaviour . . . should be written off as a travesty of personal evangelism. Impersonal evangelism would be a better name . . . rudeness of this sort dishonours God.'[3] While this activity is clearly wrong a total silence is equally reprehensible. Believers are to be alert to each situation and ready and willing to explain their faith to those who make enquiry. This does not preclude the Christian from bringing the conversation round to the subject when the situation and circumstances permit. It does put us under obligation to be prepared! It is at this point that many Christians have not given serious thought to their God-given duty.

Demanding preparation
Being prepared requires that we have a clear understanding of the subject matter. The godly man, blessed of God, meditates upon the Word of God day and night. Through such meditation he can address his soul:

> 'Bless the Lord, O my soul;
> and all that is within me, bless his holy name!
> Bless the Lord, O my soul,
> and forget not all his benefits . . .' (Psalm 103:1–2).

By reading and carefully considering the Scriptures we who believe understand how our God and Father 'has blessed us with every spiritual blessing in the heavenly places in Christ' (Ephesians 1:3). Given the opportunity the essence of David's commitment will be fulfilled:

'I will bless the Lord at all times;
His praise shall continually be in my mouth.
My soul shall make its boast in the Lord;
the humble shall hear of it and be glad'

                                        (Psalm 34:1–2).

It is necessary to think through what will be said at such a
time. 'The first principle of effective communication is to
know what you intend to communicate and then to find
the words to express it.' [4] Lines can be rehearsed, though
great care should be exercised to avoid giving a 'pat'
answer which suggests a mindless repetition more associated with sects and cults than the true children of God!
Scriptures should be committed to memory. Memorized
Scriptures aid holiness: 'Your word I have hidden in my
heart, that I might not sin against you.' They also serve in
Holy-Spirit-assisted evangelism:

'Uphold me . . . generous Spirit.
Then will I teach transgressors your ways,
and sinners shall be converted to you'

                                        (Psalm 51:12–13).

When Christians seek to live in a manner worthy of
their high calling and are empowered by the Holy Spirit
two opposite effects are evident: some people are encouraged to embrace the faith and others are deterred. In
much the same way the presence of the Holy Spirit
segregated the people in the early Christian history
recorded in Acts (Acts 5:13–14).

The principle presented by Peter, that we should be
ready to explain our faith, is one which holds good, not
just in situations of hostility, but also in the general run of
life. Our lives should show a marked difference from the
selfish and corrupt people about us. When someone asks

why we are different then there is a golden opportunity to speak about the Lord in a personal and natural manner. This is the essence of Paul's words to the Colossians: 'Walk in wisdom towards those who are outside, redeeming the time. Let your speech always be with grace, seasoned with salt, that you may know how you ought to answer each one' (Colossians 4:5–6).

Love your neighbour

Readiness to speak of our faith is part of the fulfilling of the command to love our neighbour. In loving concern for the well-being and salvation of others we shall remain alert at all times to the possibilities of a word in season. This preparedness to 'proclaim the praises of him who called you out of darkness into his marvellous light . . .' (1 Peter 2:9) will not be a burden when done in love for God and our fellow humans. When this principle is rightly understood and practised in a conscious dependence upon the Holy Spirit there should be no strain and stress, no anxiety in the presence of the unsaved. We are to be prepared! There is to be no question of partiality, we are always to be ready to speak – to the humblest as well as to the high and mighty in this world; ready in the house, ready in the street, ready in the midst of ordinary business life and the working day, ready when under extreme threat and hostility, even if like the apostle Paul we should be brought before kings and magistrates! We must be ready always to give an answer: ready before the rich and poor, educated and uneducated, intelligent and not so intelligent, for God's children are a motley band often drawn from the most unlikely quarters! (1 Corinthians 1:26–28.) In the body of Christ 'there is neither Jew nor Greek, there is neither slave nor free, there is neither male nor female' (Galatians 3:28; cf. Colossians 3:11). Paul spoke before King Agrippa and Festus. Paul spoke to his jailer and persecutor at Philippi. Be ready. No one is to be considered 'a hopeless case', though care has to be exercised that we 'do not give what is holy to the dogs; nor cast . . . pearls before swine' (Matthew 7:6). As can be seen from these words of our Lord there are those who pour such contempt upon the gospel that we are not to labour with them. The treasures of Christ are not to be presented to those who do nothing but ridicule the message and the Master.

The dignity of the church of Christ is clear. Peter writes, 'You are a chosen generation, a royal priesthood, a holy nation, his own special people, that you may proclaim the praises of him who called you out of darkness into his marvellous light . . . having your conduct honourable among the Gentiles, that when they speak against you as evil-doers, they may, by your good works which they observe, glorify God in the day of visitation' (1 Peter 2:9,12). The challenge is clear. How many believers can and do actually speak to each other, let alone to the unsaved, about the grace of God in their lives? If we cannot talk to those inside the church how shall we ever talk to those outside the church? The inane conversations which so easily pass between God's people ought to stick in their throats. God has given us a great subject for discussion and sharing together. While Christ is God's 'indescribable gift' (2 Corinthians 9:15) and we do 'rejoice with joy inexpressible and full of glory' (1 Peter 1:8), that is no reason why we should not try to describe him and try to express our joy! Every preacher knows he has an impossible task in trying to describe the magnificence of the Lord and the splendour of his grace, but that does not stop him attempting the impossible every time he stands to preach!

An explanation or defence
How many of God's people can give a reason for their

faith? The duty incumbent upon all believers is clear. A thorough-going theological dissertation is not what is required. Rather, a clear, confident testimony to the grace of God in one's own life and experience is to be forthcoming. An explanation, a defence is to be given. Why do you love God? Why do you have confidence in the work of Jesus Christ? What difference has it made to your life? What support and comfort have come to you by the Holy Spirit? What challenge, correction, instruction, come through the reading of the Scriptures? Every Christian ought to be able to express some tangible reasons for his faith.

The vast majority of the Lord's people have abdicated their responsibility to give a reason for the hope within them and now leave such things to the 'professionals'. Enthusiasm for evangelism usually means inviting the unbeliever to hear someone else speak rather than attempting to speak for oneself! The main thrust in evangelism does not lie with the preacher or pastor; it is in the hands of every man, woman and young person who admits allegiance to Christ!

Even when the responsibility to speak to the unbeliever has been faithfully accepted it is often carried out in such a way as to be quite irrelevant to those who hear. Archaic expressions and technical jargon do not confront the unsaved with the clear demands of the gospel. Forget what other Christians might think. This is no time to be concerned about the finer points of doctrine. An enquiry has been made. That puts the Christian in a strong position. He who asks a question usually listens to the answer. The Christian should try to speak about his own personal experience in language and concepts which the enquirer will understand! Writing in 1946 Percy Ruoff complained: 'Love by itself . . . is not sufficient. He who undertakes this work [speaking to others about Christ]

must have experienced for himself the truth of what he
proclaims. Far too much testimony today is, in reality,
second hand. It is served up in misunderstood phrases
and seasoned with worn-out evangelical clichés. The
hollowness and insipidness of such a witness is all too
easily exposed, and is often instinctively suspected by the
average man of the world.'[5]

What does plain speaking demand of us? Surely it is
just a case of talking naturally as we might speak about
any other topic of everyday life. The only effective way to
learn to communicate with those outside the church is to
spend time with them. There is much to learn in
observing them and listening to them. How else are we to
make the most of every opportunity? (Colossians 4:5.)

A reason for the hope

We have been 'begotten . . . again to a living hope' (1
Peter 1:3). This living hope is centred in God (1 Peter
1:21). We believe God's 'exceedingly great and precious
promises' (2 Peter 1:4). Confident that the Father 'has
blessed us with every spiritual blessing in the heavenly
places in Christ' (Ephesians 1:3) and 'looking for the
blessed hope and glorious appearing of our great God and
Saviour Jesus Christ' (Titus 2:13), we are assured that we
shall receive the end of our faith, even the salvation of our
souls (1 Peter 1:9). This is no vain hope. Our hope 'does
not disappoint, because the love of God has been poured
out in our hearts by the Holy Spirit who was given to us'
(Romans 5:5).

Hope for the hopeless

How quickly we forget! Once we were without Christ,
'having no hope and without God in the world'
(Ephesians 2:12), but now 'faith is the substance of things
hoped for' (Hebrews 11:1) and we 'rejoice in hope of the

glory of God' (Romans 5:2). We have been on both sides of the fence – without hope and with hope. Once we were hopeless; now we are hopeful. Those who are of the world need to be brought face to face with their hopelessness. All worldly hope will vanish: 'The hope of the righteous will be gladness, but the expectation of the wicked will perish' (Proverbs 10:28). 'When a wicked man dies, his expectation will perish, and the hope of the unjust perishes' (Proverbs 11:7). Those who are of the world are becoming increasingly aware of their hopelessness. Time and again we meet folk who are bewildered and crushed. Relationships are turning sour. Families are breaking up. Unemployment knocks all the drive and motivation from its victims. Hopelessness glares out on every hand. What a golden opportunity this presents for the gospel of hope!

With Messiah and with David, each believer will confidently declare, 'Therefore my heart is glad, and my glory rejoices; my flesh also will rest in hope' (Psalm 16:9). 'For you are my hope, O Lord God' (Psalm 71:5).

3. In the right spirit

It has often been said, 'You can win an argument and lose a soul!' Our manner of approach to questioners will need to be right. A gentle spirit is essential in one who would bring others to faith in Christ: 'We shall not try to violate their personalities, or exploit their weaknesses, or ride roughshod over their feelings. What we shall be trying to do, rather, is to show them the reality of our friendship and concern by sharing with them our most valuable possession.'[6] The success of our words does not depend in the final analysis upon our skill in debate or our linguistic competence. Indeed the Lord often uses the most faltering utterances to achieve great spiritual good. The apostle Peter's third requirement is to insist upon the correct manner and attitude in speaking to the unsaved.

Giving an explanation of our faith has to be done 'with meekness and fear'. When we are asked about the hope within us the answer is not to come back in a high-handed fashion. Arrogance is unseemly in a believer. We are not in the business of point-scoring or demonstrating 'one-upmanship'! God changed our hearts. God gave us faith. God gave us hope. We must not forget that the hope of salvation is all of God! Humility best befits a man who professes godliness and would share Christ with an enquirer. Dr Boreham said of Robert M'Cheyne: 'All his converts agree that it was not so much what he said as the spirit in which he said it, that lured them into the kingdom.'[7]

Robert Leighton observes, 'The Spirit of truth is withal the Spirit of meekness. The Dove that rested on that great Champion of truth, who is the Truth itself, is from Him derived to the lovers of truth, and they ought to seek the participation of it. Imprudence makes some kind of Christians lose much of their labour, in speaking for religion, and drive those further off, whom they would draw into it.'[8]

A holy fear tempers our speech. Reverence for God and respect for holy things will ensure that our words are chosen with care and graciously uttered. There is a fear too, that as we speak to others, the form of our testimony might not prejudice them against Christ! How our inadequacy is exposed at such times! Gross inability to express 'the unsearchable riches of Christ' (Ephesians 3:8) would greatly hinder the extension of the kingdom of God were it not for the unique work of the Holy Spirit. When we have done our best and presented our case as clearly and graciously as we know how, 'we are unprofitable servants. We have done what was our duty to do' (Luke 17:10).

References
1. C. John Miller, *Evangelism and Your Church*, p. 29.
2. R.C.H. Lenski, *Interpretation of Colossians, Thessalonians, Timothy, Titus and Philemon*, Augsburg Publishing House, p. 308.
3. J.I. Packer, *Evangelism and the Sovereignty of God*, IVP, p. 81.
4. John Miller, *Evangelism and Your Church*, p. 79.
5. Percy O. Ruoff, *Personal Work*, IVP, p. 34.
6. J.I. Packer, *Evangelism and the Sovereignty of God*, *p. 80*.
7. Quoted by Ruoff, *Personal Work*, p. 47.
8. *The Works of Robert Leighton*, vol. 2, p. 172.

— 10 —

Providential opportunities

All of God's people have to be ready to share their faith with unbelievers. Only a few will be called to devote all their time and energy to the spreading of the gospel. In other words, every Christian is to be prepared to be evangelistic when opportunities arise, but only some Christians are to be trained and supported as 'evangelists' who will go out to make opportunities! The confusion of these two roles has resulted in considerable anguish and guilt in the minds of many sincere Christians. An example of this is found in the student world. Christians attending college or university may feel that the pressure to make opportunities is so great that they spend far too much time on organized evangelistic outreach and not enough time on their studies. God is not honoured when students fail their exams or under-achieve because they have spent an inordinate amount of time organizing talks for fellow students.

It is quite wrong to suppose that all God's children have to be evangelists. Such thinking causes anxiety in the Christian which often manifests itself in an obsessive talking about 'religion'! The worker in the factory, office, classroom or operating theatre is there, not to evangelize, but to do a good job of work for which he will be paid. It is God's will that a man supports himself by gainful employment (2 Thessalonians 3:10) unless this is rendered impossible due to illness or the absence of work. The Lord directs the husband and father to provide for his family (1 Timothy 5:4,8). Such work is to be done to the best of his ability (Ecclesiastes 9:10). The obligation from the Lord is clear. We are to live for the praise of his glory. Such praise is achieved primarily by working well and producing good quality work. Coupled with this will be right behaviour and attitudes: responding to people and situations in a Christian manner and showing the love, joy, peace, long-suffering, kindness, goodness, faithfulness, gentleness and self-control (Galatians 5:22–23) which are the beautiful evidence of the Spirit's indwelling. Christians do not work in order to win their workmates for Christ! We work to live and provide adequately for our families and to support the work of God in its various expressions.

However, though the conversion of others is not the motive for one's employment or profession it is nevertheless a factor to be borne in mind. The Lord often puts his people in the right place at the right time in order that living contact may be made with one of his lost sheep (Luke 15:4–7). The Lord has a wonderful way of getting his own way! He achieves everything 'according to the counsel of his will' (Ephesians 1:11). He not only ensures 'that all things work together for good to those who love God' (Romans 8:28); he also works through circumstances and situations to bring his chosen people to faith in his Son.

Providential circumstances affecting evangelism

Providential circumstances influence the believer not simply for his own good (even fierce persecution is harnessed by God for the blessing of the saints) (1 Peter 1:6–7) but also for the good of others. Under God's hand persecution develops Christian character (James 1:2–4). By his grace and mercy it is also used to extend the kingdom of Christ. A typical example of this is recorded in Acts 8 immediately following the death of godly Stephen. Persecution burst out upon the church 'and they were . . . scattered throughout the regions of Judea and Samaria' (Acts 8:1).

This situation was not in the control of the church. Christians were driven out of Jerusalem under persecution. They were uprooted. They had to leave their relatives, friends, homes, work and familiar surroundings. They became, in the apostle Peter's words, the chosen strangers of the dispersion (1 Peter 1:1).

The effect of persecution

It is interesting and instructive to note the manner in which these early Christians reacted to being driven from their homes under persecution. To flee was not sinful. Our Lord instructed the early disciples: 'When they persecute you in this city, flee to another' (Matthew 10:23). This principle has often guided the godly.

God is in control of all circumstances. He is the great Lord and God, 'who made heaven and earth and the sea, and all that is in them' (Acts 4:24). He is Sovereign Lord God, the supreme Ruler! What was happening to the early Christians in Jerusalem was entirely within the providence of God.

'The steps of a good man are ordered by the Lord,
and he delights in his way.
Though he fall, he shall not be utterly cast down;
for the Lord upholds him with his hand'

(Psalm 37:24)

Persecution broke out and the people were dispersed. By this means the kingdom of God was promoted because 'those who were scattered went everywhere preaching the word' (Acts 8:4).

The triumph of the Lord

Persecution proved to be a blessing in disguise for it resulted in the spread of the gospel. Our magnificent God is able to turn circumstances round. When Satan seeks to destroy the church the Lord influences the situation and the church is strengthened and enlarged. The enlightenment of the Holy Spirit causes us to know 'the exceeding greatness of his power towards us who believe' (Ephesians 1:17,19). This godly dynamic coupled with love for God and for his Son enables Christians to witness boldly in the face of persecution (Acts 4:13,29,31; cf. John 15:20,26–27). In the early church there was 'rejoicing that they were counted worthy to suffer shame for his name' (Acts 5:41; cf. 1 Peter 4:16).

'When persecuted, they did not fight it or court martyrdom, except as a last resort, but moved on to another place. They were citizens of a kingdom and trusted implicitly in God's control over circumstances. Paul escaped Damascus in a basket (Acts 9:25), fled from Iconium to Lystra (Acts 14:6), after being stoned in Lystra went to Derbe (Acts 14:19–20), left Thessalonica at night (Acts 17:10) and used his citizenship to escape the Jews' clutches in Judea. But that the Spirit led in this mobility is clear from His directions to the church at Antioch (Acts 13:1–4), their being forbidden to speak in Asia and Bithynia (Acts 16:6–7) and the vision to stay in Corinth (Acts 18:9–11).'[1]

The providential dealings of God have considerable bearing on our evangelism. The early Christians reacted to persecution and being driven from their homes, not by complaining and grumbling, nor by challenging the wisdom, love and power of their heavenly Father, but by sharing the good news of Jesus Christ wherever they went. The sharp contrast is drawn in Acts 8, where on the one hand, Saul 'made havoc of the church' (v. 3), but on the other hand the dispersed Christians spread the gospel! 'We here see how God was turning this persecution to his own great ends. Saul thought he was crushing the Christian movement; in reality, the harder he worked to do so, the more he himself helped to spread that movement.'[2]

Wherever the persecuted Christians travelled, wherever they stayed or attempted to settle, they 'told as good news the Word' (*evangelizo* used in its ordinary sense of sharing good news, as in Luke 1:19; 2:10; 3:18, and not in the official sense of 'to preach'). Dr Martyn Lloyd-Jones popularized the view that these Christians 'gossipped the gospel'! These were ordinary Christians. They did not set themselves up as preachers but told people why they had to leave Jerusalem and in this way they testified and witnessed to their faith in Jesus Christ. They fulfilled the duty which has been laid upon all believers (1 Peter 3:15). They were driven as far as Phoenicia, Cyprus and Antioch (Acts 11:19) and they faithfully shared the gospel.

God is out there in his world!

Evangelism is not some narrowly restricted activity to be

packaged into neat little parcels labelled, 'outdoor-preaching,' 'tract distribution,' 'invitations to special meetings,' or whatever. It is an aspect of the Christian's life which influences every contact and every involvement which he has with the unbeliever. 'Get them in' has been the watchword but has had little effect. Thousands of leaflets are distributed annually. Thousands of Bibles are given away free of charge. What are the results? In terms of the hours and manpower devoted to such work there is little to show. Young Christians who begin with such enthusiasm become increasingly deflated and disillusioned by the poor response. We need to have a new and fresh look at our individual circumstances: where we live, where we work, what interests, hobbies and activities we pursue. We need to ask the question: 'Why am I here in this particular place, at this particular time, with these particular people?' What providential opportunities are opening up right here?

John came to our fellowship from a godly home in the south. He was a student at the Leicester Polytechnic. He spoke openly and graciously about his Lord. For three years he brought fellow students to meet his Christian friends. During that period he brought over thirty students under the influence of the gospel. With all of them there had been initial conversation. He was not at college to be an evangelist. He did not go round from door to door. He did not leave tracts here, there and everywhere. He was not a 'Bible-basher'. He loved God and maintained a pure witness. His love for his fellow students was obvious. He cared about people. Eight students came to faith in Christ! John had used the providential opportunities!

A believer may have taken a particular job because there was nothing else available; he may dislike the people with whom he is expected to work; the street where he lives may not be especially pleasant; his house may have become unsuited to his higher position at work; but he must not be hasty in seeking a change. Has God placed him in a strategic location with a commission: 'that you may proclaim the praises of him who called you out of darkness into his marvellous light'? (1 Peter 2:9.)

God's strategy

As Eric Wright pointed out, 'God alone has the eternal strategy at his fingertips!' There are many issues in life over which we have no control. For example, we do not choose our nationality, our parents, the location of our childhood and youth. Even when we think hard and pray earnestly before making decisions – about a partner in marriage, about the job opportunities which arise, about the purchase of a home – who knows just how much influence is being exerted from heaven? Well did the wisest king say, 'A man's heart plans his way, but the Lord directs his steps' (Proverbs 16:9).

In the providential circumstances of life over which we have little or no control the response may be pessimistic or optimistic. Either we moan, complain and grumble, or we ask, 'Why am I here?' How can I serve God best right here and now? How can I show the Lord that he really did put in the best man for the job?

How often we hear examples of God's providential dealings in evangelism! There was a young man who, while at college, was befriended by a Christian colleague who shared the gospel with him. He eventually went along with him to a preaching meeting and decided *against* believing. The young man admitted that this association had made a lasting impression on him. Three years later and a hundred miles away, he became friendly with a young lady who occasionally attended a Bible-based church. He accompanied her to a preaching meeting and his response was almost instantaneous. In a little time both were converted. Were these occurrences coincidental? The brother in Christ who first spoke about the love of God to his friend in college could not have realized the vital place he had in God's providential dealings with a sinner ordained to eternal life (Acts 13:48).

A wide view of evangelism sees every experience in the light of gospel potential. When illness strikes, unemployment hits, difficulties and disappointments arise, how good it is to be able to reflect and testify, 'I want you to know, brethren, that the things which happened to me have actually turned out for the furtherance of the gospel'! (Philippians 1:12.) Paul's imprisonment did not interrupt the extension of the kingdom of Christ; it actually achieved it!

The godly will learn from the wise man of old who said,

'Trust in the Lord with all your heart,
and lean not on your own understanding;
in all your ways acknowledge him,
and he shall direct your paths' (Proverbs 3:5–6).

References
1. Eric Wright, *Tell the World*, Evangelical Press, p. 120.
2. R.C.H. Lenski, *Interpretation of The Acts of the Apostles*, Augsburg Publishing House, p. 314.

——— 11 ———

The need for evangelists

So far we have been concerned with unplanned, spontaneous encounters under the providence of God and in the normal circumstances of life! These contacts, however, are not sufficient if the people of God are to fulfil the great commission to make disciples of all nations! (Matthew 28:19–20.) The church will not achieve her God-given task simply by responding faithfully to the providential opportunities which occur in day-to-day situations. There is a place for another, quite different approach, working alongside the first. This alternative and complementary method is through God-called, God-anointed men who function as 'evangelists'. The apostle Paul indicated that such men are part of Christ's team of men given to the church: 'He himself gave some to be apostles, some prophets, some evangelists, and some pastors and teachers, for the equipping of the saints for the work of ministry, for the edifying of the body of Christ ...' (Ephesians 4:11).

Building the true church

The edifying or building up of the body of Christ takes place in two ways. On the one hand there is the work of conversion ('The Lord added to the church daily those who were being saved', Acts 2:47). Sinners are called upon to come to Christ 'as living stones' and be built up as 'a spiritual house' (1 Peter 2:5). The church of Christ is a structure which will one day be completed. Of course, God knows the final dimensions of this spiritual building already! He knows who will be brought to salvation in Christ his Son.

The building of the body of Christ has also another aspect – that of internal growth, which is believers increasing in maturity. The two kinds of growth are really one. Together they represent Christ exercising his kingly rule ('I will build my church', Matthew 16:18). The growth of the church continues quantitively and qualitively, 'till we all come to the unity of the faith and the knowledge of the Son of God, to a perfect man, to the measure of the stature of the fulness of Christ' (Ephesians 4:13).

How does the Lord cause his Word to be spoken so that, as it is mixed with faith in the hearers (Hebrews 4:2), it causes growth? Scripture leaves us in no doubt. The Lord has made arrangements for growth through the gifts which he has given to the church. The aim of Ephesians 4 is to show the growth of the church into a mature, perfect, complete body.

That all four sets of workers – apostles, prophets, evangelists, pastors/teachers (it is more usual to unite these two as descriptive of the one office) – were committed to both forms of church growth, in quantity and quality, is abundantly clear from the Scriptures. While distinctions in function are easily observed yet there was considerable overlapping in their work.

The first two groups of men, *apostles* and *prophets*, were given to the church for the establishment of a firm Christian foundation (Ephesians 2:20). Although their offices were not permanent the church would continue to benefit from them. We depend upon their work, their teaching and example, as recorded in the Scriptures, as a basis of sound doctrine and practice. The church in our day is not to erect an alternative building nor a complementary building. There is no freedom to create a new structure on a new foundation. We are building upon the old foundation. We dare not build another. 'For no other foundation can anyone lay than that which is laid, which is Jesus Christ' (1 Corinthians 3:11). The foundation which the Lord caused to be built by his own unique apostles and prophets will stand until the end of this age.

Pastors and *teachers* are given to the church to instruct new converts, to guard all believers from spiritual dangers, to counsel them in their distress and be a constant example to the people of God (Acts 20:28).

Between the apostles and prophets on the one hand, and pastors and teachers on the other, there stand the evangelists! Evangelists have the special task of reaching out into the domain of the enemy. Indeed they should spend more time in enemy territory than among the people of God. They are responsible for spearheading the advancement of God's kingdom.

The apostles were pastors and teachers, or 'elders' (1 Peter 5:1). (The three terms 'elders,' 'pastors', or 'shepherds', and 'overseers', or 'bishops', are taken as synonymous, see Acts 20:17,28.) The work of the apostles included work as evangelists. This is why the apostle Paul is used as an example of an evangelist. Having outlined the gospel in 1 Timothy 2:5–6, Paul writes, 'for which I was appointed a preacher [a herald–proclaimer] and an apostle – I am speaking the truth in Christ and not lying –

a teacher of the Gentiles in faith and truth' (1 Timothy 2:7). 'Herald' is a descriptive term for a preaching evangelist. It is an important word which indicates the proclamation of God's truth to the unsaved.

The evangelist

The evangelist is a neglected office. Confusion reigns as to whether or not the office continued beyond the apostolic period. The issue is not simply settled by an examination of the three references to 'evangelists'.[1] Other Scriptures have great bearing upon the task of reaching the unsaved. Jesus invited the disciples with the promise: 'Come after me, and I will make you become fishers of men' (Mark 1:17). Again there is the harvesting of which our Lord spoke when he commissioned the seventy (Luke 10:2). If the apostles and seventy disciples had fulfilled the task of evangelists by reaping a full harvest there would have been no point in asking the Lord of the harvest for more labourers! There is the planting work which was done in new towns and cities (1 Corinthians 3:6–8). Skilled workers are to sow and reap, plant and water (John 4:36–38; 1 Corinthians 3:6–8). This is a continuing work in each generation. Labourers are needed. Whether they are called 'evangelists', or 'church-planters,' or 'harvesters' or 'church-builders' is of little consequence. What is important is the fact that the Bible says so much about this kind of work and it can be demonstrated as being quite distinct from the role of a pastor/teacher in the assembly of the saints.

Redressing the balance

Even where there has been concern for the continuance of the role of evangelist it has often been carried out by untrained or partially trained enthusiasts and regarded by the church as a lesser work than that of the pastor/teacher. Throughout her history the church has placed great emphasis upon the training of men for the ministry of the Word. In our own day residential colleges and non-residential training courses are available to strengthen the local church in its own training programme. While the provision of an educated ministry is laudable the need for highly educated evangelists is more urgent.

The emphasis upon ministerial training has contributed to a low view of the evangelist. The required gifts, appointment and task of an evangelist have not been clearly understood, so special training has not been provided for those who demonstrated that they had received such a calling!

The term 'evangelist' immediately conjures up a picture of Billy Graham or Don Summers. No one can deny that these two men have been greatly used by God to bring thousands to faith in Christ. However, these two men are not really evangelists in the New Testament meaning of the word. They, along with others of a similar kind, are largely reaping within the orbit of the churches. The Billy Graham organization admits that 'In the early years those making decisions were generally from the "liberal churches where they were not hearing the gospel". But now . . . more than 90% of those making decisions are from "our evangelical churches".[2] In order to substantiate the claim that these men are not functioning according to the New Testament pattern it will be necessary to examine the Scriptures and establish, as clearly as possible, the work, qualifications, calling and appointment of evangelists.

The work of an evangelist

The term 'evangelist' occurs just three times in the New

Testament. In Acts 21:8 Philip is called 'the evangelist'. In Ephesians 4:11 the ascending Christ 'himself gave some to be apostles, some prophets, some evangelists, and some pastors and teachers'. In 2 Timothy 4:5 Paul urges his young associate: 'You be watchful in all things, endure afflictions, do the work of an evangelist, fulfil your ministry.'

There are over 130 references in the New Testament to the words 'preach', 'preacher' or 'preaching'. The two basic Greek words used are *kérussō* 'to herald' and *euanggelizō* to 'evangelize' or 'preach as good news the word'. The first gives emphasis to the authority and content of the message – the announcement of reliable, trustworthy facts from God. The second gives emphasis to the nature and implication of the message, that it is 'good news'. Translations often obliterate this distinction. Romans 10 is an example. Compare verse 14, 'How shall they hear without a herald?' with verse 15: 'How beautiful are the feet of those announcing good news of peace, who bring good news of good things!' (literal translations)

A major part of the evangelist's task is to act as a herald to those who are as yet unbelievers. He announces the being, actions, demands and promises of the living God! The herald is responsible for a straightforward making known of facts. These facts concern the nature and reality of the living God, his work in creation, the sending of his Son, Jesus Christ, the atonement through the death of Christ and the raising up of the Lord Jesus from the dead, the command for all men everywhere to repent and the invitation to eternal life through faith in Christ.

Philip the evangelist was a herald, for in Acts 8:5 it is recorded: 'Philip went down to the city of Samaria and preached [heralded or announced] Christ to them.' The apostle Paul declares himself a herald. After writing about the salvation of sinners and saying that the only mediator between God and man is the man Christ Jesus, he declares his calling: 'for which I was appointed a preacher [herald] and an apostle – I am speaking the truth in Christ and not lying – a teacher of the Gentiles in faith and truth' (1 Timothy 2:5–7). He uses three different terms to describe his task. Each sphere of work is based upon the revelation of God in Christ but three distinct activities are in mind. As an evangelist he addressed the unconverted and applied the revelation to them, as an apostle he laid the foundation for the whole church and as a teacher he instructed Christians in the whole counsel of God.

Paul the evangelist

It is much easier to identify Paul's activity in New Testament times than it is to draw parallels and extract lessons for our twentieth-century situation. Wherever he travelled he usually addressed those who fell into two distinct groups. There were Jews (together with Gentile proselytes) and pagans. On arrival in a new town he was in the habit of going to the synagogue on the sabbath. As at Thessalonica Paul's objective was to reason and debate 'from the Scriptures, explaining and demonstrating that the Christ had to suffer and rise again from the dead, and saying, "This Jesus whom I preach to you is the Christ"' (Acts 17:2–3). This approach, based upon the agreed foundation of the Old Testament Scriptures, was suitable for Jews in the synagogue but most unsuitable for the pagans in society at large. With Gentiles Paul's method was quite different. His handling of the situation at Athens clearly indicates a marked difference of presentation (Acts 17:16–34). Jim Petersen draws certain conclusions: 'Notice the difference in the content of his message. He did not appeal to the Old Testament: he was more philosophical. He even quoted the Greek poets. He started witnessing in a different way . . . He began with the person of God. Then he spoke about Jesus and the resurrection. The results were meagre. "A few men became followers of Paul and believed" (Acts 17:34).'[3]

The formulation of an evangelistic approach based upon these two New Testament groups and relating them to the present day is bound to come up against insurmountable obstacles. Jewish synagogues are not generally open to evangelists! To draw parallels between the synagogue of New Testament times and institutional religion of our own day assumes that people are open to being reasoned with from the Bible. The vast majority of those who attend liberal 'churches' or 'chapels' need to be evangelized like pagans, for they have little respect for the Scriptures. The clergy have just about eradicated all confidence and love for God's Word among their people. It is as futile to quote the Bible in many chapels and cathedrals as it is to read it in the bar of a public house. The nearest parallel to the New Testament synagogue would be among the Jehovah's Witnesses, Christadelphians and Mormons, where at least there is respect for, though warped understanding of, the Word of God.

A people prepared

A number of recent writers have seen the evangelistic methods of Paul with the Jews and the Gentiles as being, in principle, a presentation to the 'prepared' and the 'unprepared' respectively. Where evangelism is successful among the Gentiles it is credited to the fact that they are Jewish proselytes sharing in the worship of God. They then concluded that evangelism is only successful among the 'prepared', that is, those who have come under the teaching of Scripture. This brings serious restrictions in understanding the work of God in the saving of souls. Cornelius and Lydia might well be described as 'prepared' Gentiles (Acts 10:1–2; 16:14), but what about the Philippian jailer? (Acts 16:27–34.) Furthermore to ascribe the small number of conversions at Athens to a lack of preparation through the absence of teaching from the Scriptures, or even worse, to blame the apostle for not working miracles, wonders and signs, is surely a terrible underestimation of God's saving power and a serious questioning of his saving wisdom!

There is no doubt that God does prepare people for confrontation leading to conversion. The Lord is as much in control of the events preceding our conversion as he is in those following our conversion. However, the preparatory work of the Holy Spirit may take many forms. The Lord is certainly not restricted to any clearly definable pattern. Hearers may respond eagerly to the Word of life, and from a human perspective little or no preparation has been done. The key feature in conversion is always the will and work of God. When pagan Greeks at Antioch were presented with the good news of the Lord Jesus Christ 'a great number believed and turned to the Lord'. No other reason is given for their conversion than that 'the hand of the Lord was with them' (Acts 11:21). A little later Barnabas joined the work there. Barnabas is described as 'a good man, full of the Holy Spirit and of faith. And a great many people were added to the Lord' (Acts 11:24). What a powerful combination – a good man, the Holy Spirit and faith! Similarly the Gentiles at Antioch in Pisidia, when they heard the truth proclaimed, 'were glad and glorified the word of the Lord. And as many as had been appointed to eternal life believed' (Acts 13:48). Again the reason is attributed to God's willing and working. Neither of these

cases fit the neat compartments which others would wish
to establish.

Unbelievers may be prepared for the gospel by the
providential workings of Almighty God. They are
prepared so that when they are confronted with the gospel
they are ready to respond. An exciting feature of evangelistic work is that people like this may be found
anywhere! The Lord may prepare the ground through a
godly relative, a Sunday School teacher, a godly neighbour
or friend, or through church attendance. Alternatively he
may prepare them by influencing their thinking through a
radio or television programme, the reading of a secular
book, magazine or newspaper, or through a catastrophe or
tragedy in their family. The means at God's disposal are
endless. Whether there has been preparation or not, it is
the Lord who opens the heart to respond to the message
(Acts 16:14). That message is to be given carefully and
prayerfully by the herald or messenger. At Iconium results
came because the evangelists, empowered by the Holy
Spirit, spoke so effectively 'that a great multitude both of
the Jews and of the Greeks believed' (Acts 14:1).

The issue that should be in question is not the degree of
preparation required for conversion but rather the form of
presentation required to suit the preparation.

The Jews who believed the Old Testament Scriptures to
be the inspired Word of God, coupled with the Gentile
proselytes (who shared that belief), were addressed on the
basis of biblical truth. Consequently Paul argued his case
from Scripture. Alternatively, the Gentiles who did not
believe the Old Testament Scriptures, many of whom
probably had no knowledge of such writings, were
addressed in a very different way. With them the apostle
began on the basis of common experience, of creation,
daily life and religious aspirations. He built his case

without quoting Scripture.

The crucial issue is not so much the preparation of the people as the preparation of the preacher and his ability to 'tune in' to the experiences and convictions of his hearers. Once contact has been established he moves them gently along until he discloses the glorious truths of the coming of Christ, his suffering, death and resurrection. These truths are then applied and a response required (Acts 17:30).

In other words, a very different evangelistic approach needs to be adopted when dealing with those totally outside the life of a Christian church. These folk have little or no prior knowledge of Christian things. They may have such wrong views that a seemingly insuperable obstacle lies in the path of the evangelist. It is futile to quote the Scriptures. As far as they are concerned the Bible has no relevance to them or authority over their lives. Are they therefore not to hear the Word of God? If they are to hear, as Scripture requires that they should, then the truth must be presented to them in a totally different way. Preaching to pagans means no quotations from Scripture. As Michael Green states, 'This is true apologetic, and also true evangelism, where the content of the gospel is preserved whilst the mode of expression is tuned to the ears of the recipients.'[4]

Proclamation

When the opportunity arises for an evangelistic address the evangelist would do well to remember the words of W.T. Shedd: 'His great work is to speak to the popular mind upon the subject of religion with a view to influence it; and therefore his oratorical efforts ought to be marked

by that practical, and, so to speak, business-like manner
which is seen in the children of this world, who, in their
generation, are oftentimes wiser than the children of
light.'[5]

A preacher prepared

Whether he is addressing those who have some knowledge
of Christian truth or those who are ignorant of even the
basic facts, the evangelist himself should be thoroughly
prepared to reason his case effectively. How many preachers who are regarded as good evangelists could face
questioning and respond with a carefully reasoned argument? The pulpit has become more than a convenient way
of allowing people to hear and see (concentration in listening is often affected by seeing); it has become a retreat,
a safe tower, protecting the occupant from the searching
questions of the audience.

A study of the words used in the promotion of the gospel
as recorded in the Acts of the Apostles is instructive. The
apostles and evangelists preached, confounded, proved,
disputed, exhorted, taught, declared good tidings, spoke
boldly, preached boldly, confirmed, discussed, showed or
demonstrated, reasoned, persuaded, testified and
strengthened. They proclaimed the truth in an outspoken,
frank, blunt, assured, free, open and plain manner. They
did not stand in a distant pulpit. They were not constantly
giving a monologue. They were engaged for the most part
in dialogue. Can you visualize them with the Scriptures
open before them, debating the points at issue, reasoning
from God's Word?

Far too much of our evangelism is based upon
monologue rather than dialogue. However, it needs a
certain kind of preparation to be effective in debate or

reasoning. An evangelist must be trained for such 'cut-and-thrust' discussion. The New Testament evangelists were persuasive preachers who were able to substantiate and argue their case in public or private discussion. When they were filled with the Holy Spirit their preaching carried a certain thrust with it (Acts 4:31).

Persuasive preaching

Paul's preaching before King Agrippa had all the ingredients of fine evangelistic preaching: ' "Having obtained help from God, to this day I stand, witnessing both to small and great, saying no other things than those which the prophets and Moses said would come – that the Christ would suffer, that he would be the first to rise from the dead, and would proclaim light to the Jewish people and to the Gentiles . . .

"King Agrippa, do you believe the prophets? I know that you do believe." Then Agrippa said to Paul, "You almost persuade me to become a Christian." And Paul said, "I would to God that not only you, but also all who hear me today, might become both almost and altogether such as I am, except for these chains"' (Acts 26:22–23, 27–29).

He proclaimed Christ as identified in the prophets of the Old Testament. He preached 'Christ crucified' (1 Corinthians 1:23). The apostle presented Jesus of Nazareth as Lord and Saviour. Using all the persuasive powers of reasoning at his disposal, he argued the case for Christ and Christianity. True, his speech and preaching 'were not with persuasive words of human wisdom', before Agrippa any more than before the people of Corinth. When with the Corinthians he was concerned rather to declare the truth 'in demonstration of the Spirit

and of power', that their 'faith should not be in the
wisdom of men but in the power of God' (1 Corinthians
2:4–5). He did not use philosophical arguments or reasoning, nor did he rely upon his ability to present truth.
Though he sought to make his message as clear as
possible, to set forth his evidence as convincingly as he
could, to entreat, exhort and plead with all the fervour of
his heart, yet he rested entirely upon the Spirit of God to
do the 'real' work. Conversion is never just one human
being convincing another human being. Human wisdom
converts no one, nor can it convey a knowledge of God (1
Corinthians 1:21). When, however, the Holy Spirit is at
work he acts 'at once in him who speaks and in him who
hears, in such a way as to make the light pass, through the
intervention of the spoken word, from the mind of the one
into the mind of the other'.[6]

Peter Masters expressed it in this manner: 'Entreaty
persuades men to cast themselves upon the mercy of God.
Entreaty gets them to search their own hearts, and
provokes them to give some explanation why they will not
turn, so that they feel the feebleness of their excuses.
Entreaty appeals to men as though this is a life and death
matter.'[7]

Clear uncompromising proclamation

Al Martin writes, 'The three things that ought to charac-
terize the communication of divine truth are: urgency,
orderliness, and directness.'[8] Mr Martin places repentance high on the list of priorities. He writes, 'One of the
clear marks of the ministries of the men whom God has
used in past days is that they all, without exception,
spelled out the necessity, the nature, and the fruits of
evangelical repentance.'[9] In this respect, as in many

others, Mr Martin follows such great men as J.C. Ryle, who commented upon our Lord's forerunner: 'John the Baptist spoke plainly about sin. He taught the absolute necessity of "repentance", before anyone can be saved; he preached that repentance must be proved by its "fruits"; he warned men not to rest on outward privileges, or outward union with the Church.'[10]

The evangelist must aim to make a man aware of what he is doing as a sinner. The seriousness of his condition must be presented plainly. He must do more than just declare the gospel. When the apostle Peter preached in the power of the Holy Spirit on the Day of Pentecost a large proportion of the gathering 'were cut to the heart' (Acts 2:37). Calvin comments, 'This is the beginning of repentance. This is the entrance to godliness, to feel grief for our sins and to be wounded by an awareness of our evildoing.'[11] It is simpler to stand before 'God-fearing' people and call them to repentance than to confront people who are totally without God and without hope in this world. The urgent need of the hour is for called, qualified, trained, competent evangelists to be supported by the church to spearhead this vital work.

References
1. Acts 21:8; Ephesians 4:11; 2 Timothy 4:5.
2. Jim Petersen, *Evangelism as a Lifestyle*, NavPress, p. 34.
3. *Ibid*, p. 47.
4. Michael Green, *Evangelism in the Early Church*, Hodder and Stoughton, p. 153.
5. William G.T. Shedd, *Homiletics and Pastoral Theology*, Banner of Truth Trust, p. 214.
6. Frederic Louis Godet, *Commentary on First Corinthians*, Kregel Publications, p. 129.
7. Peter M. Masters, 'Bringing Persuasion back into our Preaching', article in *Sword and Trowel*, May-June 1980, p. 26.

8. Al Martin, *What's Wrong with Preaching Today?* (Pamphlet), Banner of Truth Trust, p. 21.

9. *Ibid*, p. 18.

10. J.C. Ryle, *Commentary on Matthew's Gospel*, James Clarke and Co., p. 18.

11. John Calvin, *The Acts of the Apostles 1–13*, Saint Andrew Press, p. 77.

12

The appointment of evangelists

John Bunyan, in his masterpiece *The Pilgrim's Progress*, gives a powerful presentation of the man known as Evangelist. He is the one who first sets Pilgrim in the right direction and who keeps on appearing when there is danger of Pilgrim's getting off the narrow way which leads to life eternal. A singleness of mind, a thorough working knowledge of the Scriptures, coupled with an evident love for sinners, mark out this man of God, Evangelist.

It is to God's glory that we have men of Evangelist's calibre in the church today. Yet because the church has failed to evaluate the biblical data and understand the calling and appointment of evangelists many of these men are being wasted by being confined to their own local churches. They exercise their evangelistic gifts within the framework of pastoral care and the teaching ministry. As time and opportunity allow, they assist other churches in specifically evangelistic work. They live with a constant

tension: the demands of pastoral care and teaching in
their home assembly curtail their usefulness elsewhere.
Doing the work of an evangelist in other areas causes
them to be absent from the home congregations more
than they would wish. Such gifted men would be better
released from pastoral care in a local church and supported to be New Testament evangelists. We should think
positively in terms of what could be achieved if they were
sent out in small teams to establish churches in the
spiritually barren areas of our own country and of the
world.

The calling of evangelists

The apostle Paul placed great emphasis upon his own
calling by God (Romans 1:1; 1 Corinthians 1:1). His
calling as an apostle was unique in many respects,
especially in that he was 'an apostle (not from men nor
through man, but through Jesus Christ and God the
Father)' (Galatians 1:1). The resurrected Christ appeared
to Ananias at Damascus and told him about Saul of
Tarsus, who was to become the apostle Paul: 'Go, for he is
a chosen vessel of mine to bear my name before Gentiles,
kings, and the children of Israel' (Acts 9:15). Paul
received a commission to go to the Gentiles, 'to open their
eyes and to turn them from darkness to light, and from
the power of Satan to God' (Acts 26:18). Paul ack-
nowledged before King Agrippa, 'I was not disobedient to
the heavenly vision' (Acts 26:19). Those who use the
apostle Paul's experience as a blueprint for the calling of
Christian workers today will only lead themselves into
serious difficulties. As a result potential candidates for
the office of evangelist are either driven to make claims
which cannot be substantiated (voices, visions and

dreams) on the one hand, or else they fail to respond altogether through fear of presumption on the other. Both these reactions are to be avoided.

A divine calling to be an evangelist has two aspects: one subjective, the other objective. The subjective calling is the inner compulsion towards evangelism which a man senses within himself. The objective calling is demonstrated when the church acknowledges the evidence of such a calling. In New Testament times the appointment of evangelists was clearly of God. The experience at Antioch in Syria has no parallel in our own day. For there, it is said, 'As they ministered to the Lord and fasted, the Holy Spirit said, "Now separate for me Barnabas and Saul for the work to which I have called them"' (Acts 13:2). A clear revelation was given by God. The call of God through the church confirmed Barnabas and Saul in their own convictions.

Not only did the Holy Spirit call evangelists to their work and guide them by special revelation; he also used supernatural influences and visions, as, for example, in the call to Macedonia (Acts 16:6–9). Though God no longer guides us by such means he is nevertheless still directing operations. An evangelist must still be called to the work. When writing about evangelists, Paul reasoned like this: whether Jew or Gentile, '"Whoever calls upon the name of the Lord shall be saved." How then shall they call on him in whom they have not believed? And how shall they believe in him of whom they have not heard? And how shall they hear without a preacher [herald]? And how shall they preach [herald] unless they are sent?' (Romans 10:14–15.)

The church can still determine the will of God through earnest prayer and careful consideration. The men called of God will demonstrate the personality, qualifications, gifts and graces necessary for the work.

The office of an evangelist

Titus and Timothy were authorized to appoint elders in each of the churches (Titus 1:5; 1 Timothy 3:1–7,15). The qualifications for an elder (bishop, pastor, or shepherd) are listed in the Scriptures (1 Timothy 3:1–7; Titus 1:6–9). By contrast the qualifications for an evangelist are nowhere to be found. This has caused some to conclude that the office therefore no longer exists! But that is not so. Timothy and Titus were New Testament evangelists given a fine 'in-service training' by the apostle Paul.

Paul charges Timothy, 'Do the work of an evangelist, fulfil your ministry' (2 Timothy 4:5). Timothy is not being urged to be a pastor who has evangelistic zeal but an evangelist who has pastoral concern. The distinction is important. Pastors should not be expected to have more evangelistic zeal than other members of the church. Their primary function is the teaching of believers, though their preaching should reflect a deep concern to communicate with the unconverted who come into the assembly. The pastor's primary task is *inside* the church whereas the evangelist's primary task is *outside* the church!

The qualifications of an evangelist

From the examples of Paul, Barnabas, Silas, Timothy and Titus it would be fair to deduce that there are two ways of recognizing and appointing a man as an evangelist. Firstly he would have to fulfil the qualifications of an elder and function effectively in pastoral work. He would also have to demonstrate the gifts and graces which distinguish him as an evangelist, by being instrumental in bringing people to faith in the Lord Jesus Christ both by public ministry and private counsel. He would not be a young man but a mature elder whom God had already honoured as an evangelist and given proof of this in the very tangible form of Christian converts! These would form his finest 'letters of commendation' (2 Corinthians 3:1–3).

Assistants to the evangelists

The second way to become an evangelist is to be an assistant. Young men, respected and loved by brothers and sisters in their own local churches, should be separated to work alongside mature evangelists. Training should be undertaken and/or supervised by the evangelists to ensure a high level of competence in all matters relating to their work. Thus Timothy was a trainee under Paul (Acts 16:1–3).

Essential compassion

One of the most essential qualifications for an evangelist is an evident love for the lost. In speaking of evangelistic preaching Bob Sheehan makes an important point: 'While preaching must be plain, applied and lasting it must also be accompanied by a genuine love for the unconverted. The heart and emotions must be involved for we cannot hope to do men good if we do not have compassion on them in their sins.'[1]

Of the Lord Jesus it is said: 'When he saw the multitudes, he was moved with compassion for them, because they were weary and scattered, like sheep having no shepherd' (Matthew 9:36). The gentle compassion of our Lord showed itself in many circumstances: with the deaf mute (Mark 7:32–35); with the woman caught in adultery

(John 8:3–11); with the woman with the incurable haem-
orrhage (Luke 8:43–48); when he cried over Jerusalem
(Luke 19:41; Matthew 23:37) and at the tomb of Lazarus
(John 11:35). Nowhere was his gracious compassion more
evident than when he went to the cross for his friends
(John 15:13).

In listing the qualifications of a soul-winner C.H. Spurgeon brought out many of the essential qualities required:

> Holiness of character.
> A humble spirit.
> A living faith.
> Great simplicity of heart.
> Complete self-surrender to the Lord.
> Evident love for his hearers.
> Evident unselfishness.[2]

The Lord declares his own handling of the wayward
people of Israel:

> 'I drew them with gentle cords,
> with bands of love,
> and I was to them as those who take the yoke from
>   their neck.
> I stooped and fed them'

> (Hosea 11:4).

The loveliest expression of compassion and love comes
from the Saviour when he invites sinners who are
burdened and broken: 'Come to me, all you who labour
and are heavy laden, and I will give you rest. Take my yoke
upon you and learn from me, for I am gentle and lowly in
heart, and you will find rest for your souls. For my yoke is
easy and my burden is light' (Matthew 11:28–30).

The promise of God to the compassionate evangelist is
clear:

'Those who sow in tears shall reap in joy.
He who continually goes forth weeping,
bearing seed for sowing,
shall doubtless come again with rejoicing,
bringing his sheaves' (Psalm 126:5–6).

Evangelists will do well to take the words of the psalmist as their own:

'My mouth shall tell of your righteousness
and your salvation all the day,
for I do not know their limits.
I will go in the strength of the Lord God;
I will make mention of your righteousness,
    of yours only' (Psalm 71:15–16).

The pleas of the Lord come through the prophet Ezekiel: 'Say to them: "As I live," says the Lord God, "I have no pleasure in the death of the wicked, but that the wicked turn from his way and live. Turn, turn from your evil ways! For why should you die?"' (Ezekiel 33:11.)

An awareness of the sinner's doom without Christ will stir the evangelist to compassionate and sincere pleading. Charles Bridges, writing about the doctrinal preaching of the gospel states, "Simplicity, and godly sincerity" – not talent or eloquence – are the principles of our agency. One short sentence describes our system – "Christ is all and in all."[3] Sincerity and enthusiasm break through the barriers of indifference in the mind of unbelievers. While we are unable to convert them, we can at least make them think!

A capable preacher and an experienced pastor

Why Paul? Why Barnabas? Why Silas? Did Christians at

Antioch react against the decision to send the apostle
Paul on evangelistic/missionary service? There is
certainly a bad reaction in many quarters when a preacher with a gift and call to evangelize leaves a successful
field of labour in a large local church and journeys to
some distant part to plant churches where the name of
Christ is unknown. The tendency in recent years has been
to send inexperienced youths! The results, particularly
overseas, have been tragic both for the individuals themselves and for the communities in which they laboured. It
does not make any sense to send inexperienced, untried
and immature men out into evangelistic work on their
own. They cannot develop pastoral skills in a college. A
mountain-rescue team is not composed of men who have
only theoretic knowledge of the terrain, weather conditions and survival techniques! No one begins to tackle
Mount Everest after a few practice climbs up crags and
crannies in the dales. An evangelist, because of the very
demands of his calling, must have already beaten out his
theology in living situations. The most experienced and
capable evangelistic pastors and preachers should be
separated for this work.

Paul was a recognized and respected minister in a town
church. Could he not have fulfilled his calling as an
apostle to the Gentiles by staying at Antioch? Evidently
not. It was the Holy Spirit who separated Paul for the
work of an evangelist. Paul went out to build churches.
The churches he founded were encouraged to stand on
their own feet. He moved from town to town. He did not
create churches which were dependent on him. The
quality of his work was most certainly due to the influence
and presence of the Holy Spirit and yet his experience
and skill were used of God to great advantage.

Being an evangelist does not call for a unique and
dramatic testimony, but rather for ability to proclaim the

Word of God, to reason effectively from the Scriptures, to give pastoral care to seeking sinners and to establish Bible-based churches. The concern to gain a hearing from unbelievers has far too often caused Christians to favour 'personalities' for evangelistic work in preference to experienced and able preachers of the Word. The newly converted pop-star, politician or sportsman is placed on an evangelistic platform when, as a babe in Christ, he needs to learn rather than to teach!

The training of evangelists

The apostles Peter and John were described by the highly educated members of the Jewish Sanhedrin as 'uneducated and untrained' (lit. 'unlettered and ordinary') men. The fact that they had not attended a rabbinical school and yet were able to speak in a lucid and confident manner perplexed the Sanhedrin. The dilemma of the Jewish leaders was resolved only when they realized that Peter and John 'had been with Jesus' (Acts 4:13). They therefore attributed the boldness of the two fishermen to their association with our Lord, who was himself regarded as uneducated (John 7:15), and yet more than once confounded his opponents by reasoned biblical argument (Matthew 21:23–27; 22:15–22; Mark 10:2–9).

There has been a tendency in recent years for Christians to be suspicious of learning. With the powerful 'liberal' influence in our universities and theological colleges, which is constantly seeking to remove all confidence in the Bible, it is hardly surprising that an anti-intellectualism has grown up in some quarters. Sadly the many Bible colleges dotted throughout the U.K. have largely failed to meet the need for a thoroughgoing biblical training! (There are grand exceptions for which we praise God!)

While evangelists and elders need to know what liberal churchmen teach, they need to know more about what Scripture teaches! In particular evangelists need the skills to confront modern man at the level of everyday matters. Liberal theology and the influence of the German schools in scholastics are not burning issues to the vast majority of ordinary human beings. Greater care needs to be exercised in the choice of subjects to be studied.

Whether an evangelist is trained at university, theological college, Bible college, by means of correspondence tuition or is self-taught is largely immaterial. The crucial question is whether he has learned how to think, and in particular to think *biblically*.

More trained than a pastor

The New Testament office of evangelist is only for men thoroughly educated in the Scriptures! No man can be 'rightly dividing the word of truth' (2 Timothy 2:15) who is not spending hours in the study of sacred Scripture. If an elder is required to be 'able to teach' (1 Timothy 3:2) and to be so conversant with the Scriptures as to be constantly 'holding fast the faithful word as he has been taught, that he may be able, by sound doctrine, both to exhort and convict those who contradict' (Titus 1:9), then how much more the evangelist? He needs to be better trained, more highly competent and more experienced than a pastor. He is to do a planting work. He is to teach and train men with a view to their becoming elders in the churches: 'And the things that you have heard from me among many witnesses, commit these to faithful men who will be able to teach others also' (2 Timothy 2:2).

Far more attention should be paid to the specific preparation of evangelists. Men should be nurtured in doctrine, pastoral care and evangelistic skills. A number of writers have emphasized the need for better training for evangelists. Eric Wright is just one example: 'Missionaries and evangelists should be theologically better prepared, not less prepared, than pastors.'[4] Yet so little is being done! The Bible is constantly under attack. The Word of God is being belittled, undermined and derided in schools, colleges, chapels and institutional churches. Only a strong and thoroughgoing presentation of biblical truth will challenge unbelievers in our present day.

Training, equipping and supporting evangelists is a fine investment for the church of Jesus Christ to make. As Spurgeon pointed out, 'He who converts a soul, draws water from a fountain; but he who trains a soul-winner digs a well, from which thousands may drink to life eternal.'[5] In New Testament times those who planted churches returned 'strengthening the souls of the disciples, exhorting them to continue in the faith' (Acts 14:21–22). To the elders of the Ephesian Church Paul was able to declare, 'I kept back nothing that was helpful, but proclaimed it to you, and taught you publicly and from house to house, testifying to Jews, and also to Greeks, repentance towards God and faith towards our Lord Jesus Christ . . . I have not shunned to declare to you the whole counsel of God . . . Remember that for three years I did not cease to warn everyone night and day with tears' (Acts 20:20–21,27,31). Such work of declaring the whole counsel of God with a view to the firm establishment of a new local church demands a high degree of theological understanding!

'Theology is not the enemy of evangelism, but its handmaid. It is simply the systematic arrangement of biblical truth in convenient topical categories. And yet, "Most evangelists," writes Michael Green, "are not interested in theology; most theologians are not interested in evangelism."'[6]

The elder who takes his calling seriously and cares about the people of God will 'labour in the word and doctrine' (1 Timothy 5:17). Likewise the evangelist who cares for the lost will 'labour in the word and doctrine'. He will be grappling with the Word and seeking to apply it constantly to the needs of the unsaved. The church needs men who are entirely devoted 'to prayer and to the ministry of the word' (Acts 6:4). Let others shoulder responsibility for the multitude of distracting issues in church life. Evangelists and elders should be financially well supported by the churches (1 Corinthians 9:6–11; Galatians 6:6; 1 Timothy 5:17–18), and thus freed to concentrate upon the advancement and strengthening of Christ's kingdom on earth. Evangelists have plenty of work to do: prayer, the study of Scripture, the public or private declaration of the truth to the unsaved. Each aspect of the work will bear upon the others. No one sphere of operation can be omitted. Evangelists have got to know the doctrines of Scripture. They must work at being theologians! 'When evangelism is not fertilized, fed and controlled by theology, it becomes a stylized performance seeking its effect right through manipulative skills rather than the power of vision and the force of truth.'[7]

Once trained, where are these men to serve?

Evangelism and church planting

The primary task of an evangelist is to break new ground. A lively body of believers faithfully worshipping and serving God should multiply itself under the Holy Spirit of God – as outlined in the first ten chapters of this book. The work of evangelists is to bring new churches into existence, establish them upon a firm foundation, and then move on, leaving believers to get on with their work. There has to be thought given to evangelistic strategy. As Roy Joslin boldly asserts, 'The only way Paul could fulfil his commission to "carry God's name before the Gentiles" was to be a spiritual opportunist and strategist under the constraint and restraint of the Holy Spirit (Acts 16:6–10).'[8]

Evangelism has got to be approached with the same delicate balance as is seen in the approach of the apostles. It is the balance between a clear-eyed view of the providential factors at work in the world and a sensitivity to the direction of Almighty God. The example of the apostles and evangelists of the New Testament was to move from place to place planting and establishing new churches and then move on. Their intense mobility was not random or blanket evangelism, such as we often see today, but strategic Spirit-led movement to key places. Evangelists should be qualified, trained and experienced, then sent out by the church or churches to barren areas in key locations. Their task is to make Christ known. They are to determine to know nothing 'except Jesus Christ and him crucified', so that the faith of converts may not rest 'upon the wisdom of men but in the power of God' (1 Corinthians 2:2,5). The men of the New Testament did not preach about their own conversion, their own faith, their own repentance, or describe blessings they had received. 'We must keep the delicate balance of Christ and the apostles who did not preach bread, or healing, or success but repentance, faith and costly discipleship.'[9]

Paul gives a good principle for an evangelist: 'I have made it my aim to preach the gospel, not where Christ was named, lest I should build on another man's foundation, but as it is written: 'To whom he was not announced, they shall see; and those who have not heard shall understand' (Romans 15:20–21; cf. Isaiah 52:15).

John Wesley is reputed to have said, 'I love a commodious room, a soft cushion and a handsome pulpit, but field preaching saves souls.' His own preference was comfort and warmth, but he had an overriding concern for the salvation of sinners. To reach the miners in Bristol the preachers were out at five in the morning. Evangelists should be out there among the people. They should be wherever people can be drawn together to hear and to discuss the faith which is in Christ.

The apostle Paul took his Christian liberty seriously and used it responsibly to reach unbelievers. His watchword was, 'That I might by all means save some.' And his reason: 'This I do for the gospel's sake' (1 Corinthians 9:22–23). Great flexibility, great mobility, great urgency – and, God willing, great results!

Planting Christians and planting churches

One of the many weaknesses in modern evangelistic strategy is the failure to establish those who profess conversion in suitable churches. The New Testament approach was to work in a community until a number of people were converted. These new converts would be drawn together, regularly instructed and become a newly planted church. To plant churches is to plant new Christians into new churches. There are four related activities: sowing, reaping, planting and watering. Sowing is the indiscriminate proclamation of the Word of God (see the parable of the sower, Mark 4:3–8, 14–20). Reaping is bringing sinners to a point of faith in Christ Jesus (see the teaching of the Lord Jesus while at Sychar in Samaria, John 4:35–38). Often with reaping it is others who have done the hard work (John 4:38). Planting is the gathering together of new converts and establishing them into a church body. This is a much neglected labour! Watering is 'developing the church already founded'.[10]

The blessed man of Psalm 1, who meditates on the Word of God day and night, is

> 'like a tree
> planted by the rivers of water,
> that brings forth its fruit in its season,
> whose leaf also shall not wither' (Psalm 1:3).

The Good Shepherd leads his sheep 'beside the still waters' (Psalm 23:2). And the call of the Holy Spirit and the church is 'Let him who thirsts come. And whoever desires, let him take the water of life freely' (Revelation 22:17).

The evangelist has a great work for a great God with a great gospel. He is responsible for sowing, reaping, planting and watering in order that new churches rise up to the glory of God in the barren and deserted areas of our nation and our world.

> 'The wilderness and the wasteland shall be glad for
>   them,
> and the desert shall rejoice and blossom as the rose;
> it shall blossom abundantly and rejoice,
> even with joy and singing . . .
> They shall see the glory of the Lord,
> the excellency of our God' (Isaiah 35:1-2).

References
1. R.J. Sheehan, 'Applicatory Preaching!', *Reformation Today*, No. 70, Nov-Dec. 1982, p. 29.
2. C.H. Spurgeon, *The Soul-Winner*, Pilgrim Publications, pp. 43–44.

3.   Charles Bridges, *The Christian Ministry*, Banner of Truth
     Trust, p. 257.
4.   Eric Wright, *Tell the World*, Evangelical Press, p. 41.
5.   C.H. Spurgeon quoted by Percy O. Ruoff, *Personal Work*,
     IVP, p. 73.
6.   Quoted by Eric Wright, *Tell the World*, p. 39.
7.   J.I. Packer, *What is Evangelism – Theological Perspectives of
     Church Growth*, Presbyterian and Reformed, p.91.
8.   Roy Joslin *Urban Harvest*, Evangelical Press, p. 92.
9.   Eric Wright, *Tell the World*, p. 56.
10. Fredric Louis Godet, *Commentary on First Corinthians*, p. 174.

— 13 —

Church growth

The growth of the true church of Jesus Christ is an absolute certainty!

In the midst of all the confusion of doctrine and experiences, and often in spite of the lack of spirituality in believers, the kingdom of God is going to progress and grow. Additional citizens will be incorporated into the kingdom but it will not be without struggle and difficulty (Matthew 11:12). The devil will try his utmost to snatch the truth away from many minds to stop it taking root in the heart (Mark 4:15). He will plant false disciples among the true 'sons of the kingdom' (Matthew 13:38). But in spite of the variety and ferocity of Satan's attacks the promise of our Lord stands sure: 'I will build my church, and the gates of Hades shall not prevail against it' (Matthew 16:18).

In the early days of our Lord's ministry he was followed by very large crowds. Some seriously considered him as 'the Prophet' promised through Moses (John 6:14; cf. Deuteronomy 18:15–16,18–19), though their understan-

ding of the predictions was confused. Others viewed him
simply as a miracle worker or even just as 'a meal ticket'
(John 6:26).

The popularity of Jesus Christ

The Lord was popular with the masses for 'the common
people heard him gladly' (Mark 12:37). However, care
must be exercised in determining just what this meant.
To suggest that our Lord's teaching method and use of
language were the key to his popularity, as a number of
modern writers have done, is to misrepresent the biblical
record. Our Lord was not the easiest teacher to
understand. His dealings with Nicodemus, the woman of
Samaria and the Syro-Phoenician woman (John 3; 4;
Matthew 15:21–28) serve to illustrate the complexity of
his approach. It was by no means straightforward.
Though his approach was always gracious and the ends
beneficial to each of the parties concerned, yet he could
not be described as a 'simple' preacher. 'All these things
Jesus spoke to the multitude in parables; and without a
parable he did not speak to them, that it might be fulfilled
which was spoken by the prophet, saying: "I will open my
mouth in parables; I will utter things which have been
kept secret from the foundation of the world"' (Matthew
13:34–35; cf. Psalm 78:2). Our Lord did not set out to be
understood easily by the masses. Indeed he clearly stated
that he exercised discrimination with regard to imparting
knowledge: 'When he was alone, those around him with
the twelve asked him about the parable. And he said to
them, "To you it has been given to know the mystery of
the kingdom of God; but to those who are outside, all
things come in parables, so that 'Seeing they may see and
not perceive, and hearing they may hear and not

understand; lest they should turn, and their sins be forgiven them"' (Mark 4:10–12).

Jesus not only taught in parables, which are difficult for mature believers to understand, let alone the outsider, but he also taught such profound truth that it is hardly surprising that so many were offended by him. If Jesus had not insisted upon teaching 'the truth, the whole truth and nothing but the truth' he could have maintained a very large following (John 6:60; cf. v. 66). Popularity did not 'turn his head' for he was constantly aware of the true nature of his hearers. He 'had no need that anyone should testify of man, for he knew what was in man' (John 2:25). He took great pains to discourage his disciples from being impressed by large gatherings. Large congregations do not necessarily mean enlargement of the spiritual kingdom.

The Lord's relationship with the people of Israel does not allow for parallels to be drawn with the church's relationship to the outsider today. The whole history of Israel and the promises of God to that people make comparisons with our situation impossible. The Lord saw very little 'fruit' from his labour during his own lifetime! The Christian church had an insignificant beginning but the Saviour promised success in gospel work. His church was to become a powerful force in the world. The mustard seed was to grow into an impressive tree (Matthew 13:32).

The parables

It is important to understand the context in which the parable of the mustard seed was given. There were great crowds following Christ but few were to prove to be real Christians. Curiosity, passing interest and selfish desires for health or food all motivated some of those who

composed the multitudes. Jesus spoke to them in parables, beginning with the parable of the sower.

Jesus taught the parable of the sower in order to warn
the one 'who has ears to hear' (Mark 4:9) to take care how
he responds to the Word of life. It places upon the hearer
the onus of responsibility for unbelief and a failure to
enter into salvation. It is not the preacher (the sower – in
this case the Lord Jesus Christ), who is at fault. It is not
the quality of the seed (the Word of God) which is
suspect. The fault lies in the condition of the human
heart. The parable is not only a warning to those who hear
the gospel. It also teaches disciples why relatively few
people actually respond whole-heartedly to the gospel.

Following the parable of the sower, Jesus taught the
parable of the wheat and tares. Here our Lord introduced
another element. He warns of an insidious danger and
therefore brings a more searching word. The tares among
the wheat are the further hindrances suffered by the
kingdom of God. False Christians, suspected but not
exposed, are sown in the congregation of the church of
Jesus Christ by the great enemy Satan!

At this stage the close disciples of the Lord could be
forgiven for feeling thoroughly depressed. If the human
heart is so resistant to the Word of God, if Satan is so
crafty and powerful, then what hope has the church of
success? What is the likelihood of the church growing? In
order to avoid the natural inclination to lose heart, the
Lord teaches two parables which illustrate the
phenomenal growth of the kingdom: the parable of the
mustard seed and the parable of the leaven. These
parables show that the church will grow. From its insignificant beginnings it will become a potent force in the
world.

The kingdom will survive against all the odds. In spite
of all the losses as a result of devilish interference and the

sowing of spurious seed, in spite of all the hindrances through human indifference, hypocrisy and deceit, Jesus Christ will build his church. The church will grow. At the end of this present age Christ Jesus will have a large church: 'a great multitude which no one could number, of all nations, tribes, peoples, and tongues' (Revelation 7:9).

> See how great a flame aspires,
> Kindled by a spark of grace!
> Jesu's love the nations fires,
> Sets the kingdoms on a blaze.
>
> (Charles Wesley)

A careful and detailed study of the parable of the mustard seed should fill every believer with positive optimism.

A tiny seed: a mighty tree

The mustard seed, so small and insignificant, is sown, germinates and grows into a mighty tree which is most imposing and influential. The parable contains two major truths. The first truth is that the kingdom of God will grow from very small beginnings to become a mighty organism in the end. The second is that the kingdom of God has an unimpressive, apparently inconsequential, commencement and yet will become a most important influence for good in the world. Small becomes large; insignificant becomes influential. These are the promises communicated through the parable of the mustard seed. The kingdom of God will grow and by its very nature will invite attention and make its presence felt in a very beneficial way. Let us take a closer look at the parable. 'The kingdom of heaven is like a mustard seed, which a man took and sowed in his field, which indeed is the least of all the seeds; but when it is grown it is greater than the herbs and becomes a tree, so that the birds of the air come and nest in its branches' (Matthew 13:31).

The garden in the field

'The field (Luke has 'garden') is the world, which is God's because he made it although sin has filled it with weeds, briars and stones. Luke seems to have a more specific sense in mind. Christ was planted in the world by being planted in the garden of Israel; salvation for the world is 'of the Jews' (John 4:22). By special cultivation God made Israel his garden.'[1]

Israel – the prepared garden

> 'My Well-beloved has a vineyard
> on a very fruitful hill.
> He dug it up and cleared out its stones,
> and planted it with the choicest vine . . .
> For the vineyard of the Lord of hosts is the house of
>   Israel,
> and the men of Judah are his pleasant plant'
>
> (Isaiah 5:1–2,7).

> 'You have brought a vine out of Egypt [from
>   slavery];
> you have cast out the nations, and planted it.
> You prepared room for it,
> and caused it to take deep root,
> and it filled the land.
> The hills were covered with its shadow,
> and the mighty cedars with its boughs.

> She sent out her boughs to the Sea (Mediter-
> ranean),
> and her branches to the River (Euphrates).
> Why have you broken down her hedges,
> so that all who pass by the way pluck her fruit?
> The boar out of the woods uproots it,
> and the wild beast of the field devours it.
> Return, we beseech you, O God of hosts;
> look down from heaven and see,
> and visit this vine and the vineyard which your right
>   hand has planted,
> and the branch that you made strong for yourself
> (Psalm 80:8-15).

'Thus says the Lord God; "I will take also one of the highest branches of the high cedar and set it out. I will crop off from the topmost of its young twigs a tender one, and will plant it on a high and prominent mountain. On the mountain height of Israel I will plant it; and it will bring forth boughs, and bear fruit, and be a majestic cedar. Under it will dwell birds of every sort; in the shadow of its branches they will dwell. And all the trees of the field shall know that I, the Lord, have brought down the high tree and exalted the low tree, dried up the green tree and made the dry tree flourish; I, the Lord, have spoken and have done it"' (Ezekiel 17:22-24).

The seed is Christ

The fact that botanists know many seeds that are even smaller than the mustard seed is irrelevant to the illustration. The Lord is speaking about the seeds that were planted in ordinary gardens. The comparison between the tiny seed and the huge tree becomes all the more striking when we see that this mustard kernel represents Christ himself, from whose death the vast kingdom grows.

> 'For he shall grow up before him as a tender plant,
> and as a root out of dry ground.
> He has no form or comeliness,
> and when we see him,
> there is no beauty that we should desire him'
>
> (Isaiah 53:2).

This was fulfilled in the babe of Bethlehem. From a carpenter's home, in a despised corner of the world, came a teacher who gathered together a handful of unlettered, ordinary disciples. This same man in his early thirties fell into the hands of his enemies and died a wretched death among criminals. What could be less impressive? What could be more insignificant? After such high hopes engendered in the hearts and minds of the disciples, upon his premature death all appeared lost (Luke 24:21).

The teaching of the Lord as to the success of his kingdom finds ready proof in the Acts of the Apostles. The disciples of Christ are privileged to see greater developments than the Master himself experienced while on earth. He predicted their success. For he said to them, 'Most assuredly, I say to you, he who believes in me, the works that I do he will do also; and greater works than these he will do, because I go to my Father' (John 14:12). No one has ever done greater miracles in the natural realm than those performed by the Lord Jesus Christ! By these he proved his unique Messiahship (Matthew 11:3–5). By miraculous signs he is demonstrated to be the Christ of God and the Son of God, so that those who believe in him might have eternal life (John 20:31; cf. Acts 2:22).

Jesus predicts, however, that his disciples will accomplish more than he did. The miracles of healing and power in the physical domain are eclipsed by the miracles of healing and power in the spiritual domain. The disciples were to see far more conversions than their Master! Not that he was uninvolved. Their success is in reality the Lord's success through them, for it is due to his work at Calvary and his commissioning of the Holy Spirit to the great work of gospel outreach.

The key to John 14:12 is the last clause, 'because I go to the Father'. The Holy Spirit's work in the world in a new and dynamic manner was dependent upon the victory of the Son of God at Calvary and his subsequent glorification (John 7:39). Pentecost was the obvious time for the outpouring of the Holy Spirit. Christ had died at Passover, risen on the festival of 'firstfruits' (Leviticus 23:10–11; cf. 1 Corinthians 15:20) and ascended to heaven (Acts 1:9). Ten days later was the Feast of Pentecost. Under the Old Covenant Pentecost was the celebration of the main harvest gathering. Spiritually fulfilled in the new covenant, it is the beginning of Christ's great harvest ingathering of the saved of all nations.

The seed was sown

The mustard seed was taken and sown in the field (Matthew 13:31). This removes any suggestion of an element of chance. The seed is not pictured as falling from the beak of a bird or as being driven willy-nilly by the breeze. God sent his Son into the world and thereby 'planted' him in the field. 'When the fulness of the time had come, God sent forth his Son, born of a woman, born under the law, to redeem those who were under the law, that we might receive the adoption as sons' (Galatians 4:4–5). When Christ came into the world he said to the

Father, 'A body you have prepared for me . . . Behold, I have come . . . to do your will, O God' (Hebrews 10:5-7).

The seed must die

As Christ had earlier proclaimed to the Greek visitors, 'Most assuredly, I say to you, unless an ear of wheat falls into the ground and dies, it remains alone; but if it dies, it produces much grain' (John 12:24). Within seven days the Lord fulfilled his prophecy. He was the seed dying to give life and produce fruit! By his death he produced much fruit: 'He shall see the fruit of the travail of his soul and be satisfied' (Isaiah 53:11 RSV). The visit of the Greeks to see Jesus marked the prelude for the fulfilment of Daniel's vision.

> 'I was watching in the night visions,
> and behold, one like the Son of Man,
> coming with the clouds of heaven!
> He came to the Ancient of Days,
> and they brought him near before him.
> Then to him was given dominion
> and glory and a kingdom,
> that all peoples, nations, and languages should
> serve him.
> His dominion is an everlasting dominion,
> which shall not pass away,
> and his kingdom the one
> which shall not be destroyed' (Daniel 7:13–14).

Through death the Lord Jesus 'destroys him who had the power of death, that is, the devil' (Hebrews 2:14). He brings liberty to the captives. A great potent force is released, breaking Satan's hold upon the nations of the earth. The risen Christ is symbolically portrayed as seated on a white horse riding across the countries of the world. He is traversing the globe 'conquering and to conquer' (Revelation 6:2). All those slain with his two-edged sword (Revelation 1:16; cf. Hebrews 4:12) willingly and gladly join his army (Psalm 110:3). In a single historical event we discover God 'has delivered us from the power of darkness and translated us into the kingdom of the Son of his love' (Colossians 1:13).

If Christ had not died to give himself for the church and to the church he would have remained 'alone, incommunicable and in mysterious exclusiveness apart'.[2] Having died, Christ produces plenty of fruit: 'He shall see his seed, he shall prolong his days, and the pleasure of the Lord shall prosper in his hand' (Isaiah 53:10).

Success is assured!

There are times when the mustard tree looks weather-beaten and leafless. The church of Jesus Christ is not always full of life and vigour. During the periods of winter when growth is slow and imperceptible believers reassure themselves through God's Word that none shall destroy this mighty tree. Its glory lies in the fact that God is watching over it in love. 'For who has despised the day of small things?' (Zechariah 4:10). Winter does not last for ever. The overriding promise to the church is success!

We want to see the kingdom of God succeeding in the lives of sinners. We need not feel apologetic when we long for conversions and rejoice with the angels of heaven when a sinner repents! (Luke 15:10.) We preach the gospel believing it to be 'the power of God to salvation' (Romans 1:16). We expect to see people converted. When the church sees spiritual success then we rejoice and

thank God. When we do not see success we mourn and
seek God. There is little consolation in being faithful if we
are not also being fruitful!

'Our great object of glorifying God is . . . to be mainly
achieved by the winning of souls. We *must* see souls born
unto God. If we do not, our cry should be that of Rachel:
"Give me children, or I die." If we do not win souls, we
should mourn as the husbandman who sees no harvest, as
the fisherman who returns to his cottage with an empty
net, or as the huntsman who has in vain roamed over hill
and dale. Ours should be Isaiah's language uttered with
many a sigh and groan – "Who hath believed our report?
and to whom is the arm of the Lord revealed?" The
ambassadors of peace should not cease to weep bitterly
until sinners weep for their sins![3]

Paul expected fruit for his labours

Paul's longing to visit Rome was coloured by his desire to
see conversions. He wrote to the saints there: 'I do not
want you to be unaware, brethren, that I often planned to
come to you (but was hindered until now), that I might
have some fruit among you also, just as among the other
Gentiles' (Romans 1:13). Paul wished to see some fruit of
his ministry among them. This was his great desire
everywhere he went in the service of Christ. The Lord
Jesus told his apostles, 'I chose you and appointed you
that you should go and bear fruit' (John 15:16). Paul was
zealous to see this promise fulfilled wherever he travelled.

Writing from Ephesus the apostle Paul declared, 'A
great and effective door has opened to me' (1 Corinthians
16:9). And as Jim Packer points out, 'He knew that if
Christ had opened the door for him to make known the
gospel in a place, that meant that it was Christ's purpose

to draw sinners to himself in that place.'[4] Even during his evangelistic preaching Paul was aware of the power of God in conversion. Among the people of Thessalonica he experienced an assurance within himself of the Holy Spirit's working as he preached the gospel (1 Thessalonians 1:5). This served to convince him of their 'election by God' (v. 4). Coupled with this was their receiving 'the word in much affliction' though also 'with joy of the Holy Spirit' (v. 6). The Holy Spirit was working in both the evangelist (Paul was conscious of God's presence and power within himself) and in the evangelized (they heard, believed and accepted the Word).

What great comfort the Lord gave to Paul when he laboured in Corinth! 'Do not be afraid, but speak, and do not keep silent; for I am with you, and no one will attack you to hurt you; for I have many people in this city' (Acts 18:9–10). The knowledge of God's protection is a wonderful disclosure but that which would give Paul most delight and pleasure is that final assurance: 'I have many people in this city.' This reassurance to Paul in his gospel work is a reflection of God's commission to Joshua in his work of leadership: 'This Book of the Law shall not depart from your mouth, but you shall meditate in it day and night, that you may observe to do according to all that is written in it. For then you will make your way prosperous, and then you will have good success. "Have I not commanded you? Be strong and of good courage; do not be afraid, nor be dismayed; for the Lord your God is with you wherever you go"' (Joshua 1:8–9).

'Then you will have good success!'

References
1. R.C.H. Lenski, *The Interpretation of St Matthew's Gospel*, Augsburg Publishing House, p. 528.

2. Rudolf Stier, *The Words of the Lord Jesus* T & T Clarke, vol. 6, p. 83.
3. C.H. Spurgeon, *Second Series of Lectures to my Students*, p. 180.
4. J.I. Packer, *Evangelism and the Sovereignty of God*, IVP, p. 116.

— 14 —

Evangelism and social concern

The parable of the mustard seed teaches more than just the immense growth of the kingdom of God. Creatures which gain shelter, protection and security are to be found within the framework of that great tree, for 'the birds of the air come and nest in its branches' (Matthew 13:31). In this simple and descriptive way our Lord brings attention to the benefits which many unconverted people derive from the church. R.C.H. Lenski interprets the expression 'birds of the air': 'Since the mustard tree itself is the kingdom, all who belong to the kingdom are part of this tree. The wild birds who also go tenting in it are not members of the kingdom but men in general who find the church beneficial and enjoy its beneficient influence in the world.'[1] Although the main lesson of the parable is the unobstructed growth of the church into a mighty company of believing people, yet our Lord takes into account the good influence that the church will bring upon others who do not come to faith.

When we raise the subject of social concern the alarm bells will be ringing for brethren who rightly fear an introduction of the 'social gospel.' Our first step must be to establish the biblical basis of the church's role in the community. Then we must face up to the implications of that role. In the final part of the chapter the relationship between evangelism and social concern will be examined.

The foundation for social concern

Our Lord summed up all law in two commandments: 'You shall love the Lord your God with all your heart, with all your soul, and with all your mind,' and 'You shall love your neighbour as yourself' (Matthew 22:37,39).

Worship, prayer, the study of Scripture, holiness, godliness, obedience, service, whatever we do, whatever we are, all personal spiritual life, all stems from the first commandment: the love of God with all our being. This whole-hearted love for God is, furthermore, the motive for the second commandment. Love for our neighbour stems from our love for God. The second commandment embodies our duty towards men. The Lord does not present an impossible command like 'Love everybody', for that would be entirely beyond our scope. He defines it in terms of those with whom we come into some form of contact – by arrangement, planning or 'by chance'.

The Good Samaritan

R.C. Trench in his classic work on the parables of our Lord comments upon the expression 'by chance' used by our Lord in the parable of the Good Samaritan (Luke 10:31):

'By coincidence, we might say, by that wonderful falling-in of one event with another, which often seems chance to us, being indeed the mysterious weaving-in, by a higher hand, of the threads of different men's lives into one common woof. That hand brings the negative pole of one man's need into contact with the positive of another man's power to help, one man's emptiness into relation with another's fulness. Many of our summonses to acts of love are of this kind, and they are those, perhaps, which we are most in danger of missing, through a failing to see in them this ordering of God.'[2]

Instead of discriminating between one human being and another (as the lawyer had expected), our Lord forcefully teaches him (and us) to have a neighbourly attitude. What could be more convincing that loving concern for the welfare of other human beings goes beyond the boundary of the church than the parable of the Good Samaritan? (Luke 10:25–37.) No further proof is needed that loving concern is shown in very practical ways. True neighbourliness is caring for someone whom you come across who does not share your religious convictions! As far as it is in our power we have the responsibility to demonstrate practical love towards other human beings.

What is social concern?

Social concern is simply a loving interest in the well-being of people – as people! The apostle Paul encouraged the Christians at Galatia, 'Do good to all, especially to those who are of the household of faith' (Galatians 6:10). When he writes, 'especially to those who are of the household of faith' it does not weaken or lessen our responsibility towards all men, women and children. Concern for people means being sympathetic when they are in great distress, trying to help when they are in great difficulties, lending a hand when they are in grave danger. To love people is to love them *as people*. The church has to care about people who are unemployed. We have to be concerned about people who are neglected, ill and lonely. It should be natural for believers to be moved with compassion at the plight of youngsters and children being battered by their parents, of elderly folk being terrified out of their minds, of women being molested and abused and of children, young people and older folk gripped by drugs or alcohol!

But how are we to respond? Should we keep ourselves exclusively to 'religious' matters? Are we to preach salvation, talk about the Lord, pray for sinners to be saved – and do no more? In other words, is there a God-instigated and God-honouring social concern laid upon us which moves us to take further steps?

The example of Christ

Our Saviour was often moved with compassion. His compassion was expressed in concern for the health and 'wholeness' of the people. At times there were clear overtones of spiritual concern for the people: 'And Jesus went about all the cities and villages, teaching in their synagogues, preaching the gospel of the kingdom, and healing every sickness and every disease among the people. But when he saw the multitudes, he was moved with compassion for them, because they were weary and scattered, like sheep having no shepherd' (Matthew 9:36). This experience prompted the Lord to encourage the disciples to earnest prayer for more workers in the harvest field (v. 38).

At other times, as in the feeding of the five thousand, his concern was expressed for their bodily needs (though his dealing with the spiritual need eventually goes far beyond one simple meal – see John 6:26–58). The practical result of our Saviour's compassion was bread and fish for everyone, with plenty to spare: 'Then Jesus called his disciples to him and said, "I have compassion on the multitude, because they have now continued with me three days and have nothing to eat. And I do not want to send them away hungry, lest they faint on the way"' (Matthew 15:32). At times the Lord's concern is for their physical well-being. At other times his concern is for their spiritual well-being. However, there are many occasions when it is impossible to see a clear distinction between the physical and the spiritual. Indeed, we must conclude that the Lord responded to human suffering in whatever form it was expressed – mental disorder, demon possession, physical illness, or spiritual blindness. When confronted by the woman who had suffered a severe haemorrhage for twelve years the Lord 'had compassion on her' (Luke 7:13). The Lord showed compassion on the Gadarene demoniac (Mark 5:19). Loving compassion moved the Saviour to alleviate suffering wherever it confronted him! The Saviour's compassion pushed relentlessly over all barriers. 'The blind receive their sight and the lame walk; the lepers are cleansed and the deaf hear; the dead are raised up and the poor have the gospel preached to them' (Matthew 11:5).

At Caesarea Peter gave testimony of the Lord Jesus that he 'went about doing good and healing all who were oppressed by the devil, for God was with him' (Acts 10:38). Having a true social concern for unconverted people is to follow the Master's example!

The apostles and the seventy and social concern

Christ gave the twelve apostles a commission: 'Preach,

saying, "The kingdom of heaven is at hand." Heal the sick, cleanse the lepers, raise the dead, cast out demons' (Matthew 10:7–8). To the seventy he gave the instruction to declare the kingdom of God, heal the sick and cast out demons (Luke 10:1,9,17). Our Lord was concerned about the physical, emotional, intellectual and spiritual state of the people. The healings that were performed and the demons that were cast out are not to be thought of as 'party tricks' to attract attention, nor as a clever ploy to soften the audience. Other miracles could have been performed had the purpose been to impress. Jesus had a greater motive. He gave his servants power to alleviate suffering of the mind, of the body and of the spirit. Although we do not now possess the selfsame powers known in the early Christian church, yet we still have the solemn duty to bring what assistance and help we can to the needs of our fellow men.

There are occasions, in God's providence, when acts of mercy, kindness and compassion open the way for the gospel. In Macedonia and Achaia it was the impact of transformed lives, demonstrated in 'works of faith' and 'labours of love', which paved the way for gospel presentation (1 Thessalonians 1:3,8). But it must not be thought that this is the motive behind such loving action! We love God because God loves us. We love Christians because God loves us. And we love others because God loves us.

A Christian church which is spiritual and outward-looking in love is a most powerful influence in evangelistic work. To be able to point to the man who went about 'doing good' and to the church which is seeking to follow in his footsteps 'doing good' has immediate relevance for all who listen to the Christian challenge.

The sheep and goats

The division of mankind when the Son of God comes in his

glory will be done on the basis of true love practically demonstrated. The parable of the sheep and goats indicates who will be given the invitation: 'Come, you blessed of my Father, inherit the kingdom prepared for you from the foundation of the world.' It will be those of whom Christ will be able to say, 'I was hungry and you gave me food; I was thirsty and you gave me drink; I was a stranger and you took me in; I was naked and you clothed me; I was sick and you visited me; I was in prison and you came to me' (Matthew 25:31,34–36).

Clearly our Lord is expressing, in practical terms, the same message as 'Love one another as I have loved you' (John 15:12). The point at issue in the parable is how well believers have responded to the needs of other believers. In serving 'one of the least' in the body of Christ we serve Christ himself (Matthew 25:40). The apostle John wrote, 'We know that we have passed from death to life, because we love the brethren' (1 John 3:14).

Practical love is to be shown to brothers and sisters in the church of Christ, not just in the limited sphere of our own local church but throughout the community, nation and world as and when we have opportunity. But there is more. We are exhorted to 'do good to all' (Galatians 6:10). We are urged to imitate God and walk in love (Ephesians 5:1–2). Christ leaves us in no doubt as to the breadth of that love and benevolence. 'Love your enemies, bless those who curse you, do good to those who hate you, and pray for those who spitefully use you and persecute you, that you may be sons of your Father in heaven; for he makes his sun to rise on the evil and on the good, and sends rain on the just and on the unjust' (Matthew 5:44–45). What better motive for social concern could there be than to be 'like the Father'? We have to do good even to those who hate us!

The letter of James

James brings forth stern criticism of a religion which has no practical outworking to it: 'Pure and undefiled religion before God and the Father is this: to visit orphans and widows in their trouble, and to keep oneself unspotted from the world' (James 1:27).

He goes on to show that partiality expressed on the basis of wealth or dress is sin (James 2:9). Speaking pious words to a hungry brother or sister without any practical assistance is futile (James 2:15–16). The corruption of the rich living in pleasure and luxury and their dishonest and callous treatment of employees are likewise condemned in the strongest possible terms (James 5:1–6).

The book of James is loaded with ethical teaching appropriate for the market-place – Common Market, stock-market or fish-market! Francis Schaeffer, too, has some pointed remarks to make about those who generate and use wealth. He speaks of the 'compassionate use of wealth', by which he means 'making it with justice; and then using it with real compassion'[3]. For well over half a century Christians have suffered from severe 'cognitive dissonance', by which I mean, a division of life into neat little compartments, such as, 'home and family,' 'work and finance,' 'friendship and leisure,' 'worship and devotions,' etc. Great care is then taken to avoid allowing one area to spill over into another. The most serious effect of this mentality is that spiritual values and the influence and control of the Word of God have not been given their rightful place in *all* areas of life. Christians have understood the influence of the Bible on matters of worship and personal devotion – though not always to the degree which honours God – yet the world of the family, business, politics and social care has been largely untouched. Indeed many professing believers might even consider the Scriptures to be irrelevant to such areas of life!

According to James social concern coupled with appropriate social action is a necessary part of Christian commitment. A man may give away thousands of pounds but if he earned it by cruelty, cheating, violence or injustice his charity will rot with him. Furthermore it is extremely difficult to evangelize those who harbour resentment against Christians as a result of such dealings.

The mustard tree is growing

It is always good to look at history and note the beneficial influences exerted by individual Christians and the Christian church as a whole. The church's growth and influence in our own land has been quite marked. In the past the church exerted a beneficial influence upon our society. Even non-Christian historians readily admit the good effects of true Christianity.

M.St J. Parker and D.J. Reid, writing in their sociological textbook *The British Revolution 1750–1970*, make the following observations: 'Religion was in fact a force of major social importance throughout this period.' 'Men of conscience who looked around them at the state of the poor, particularly as the Industrial Revolution made its effects felt, were often unhappy at the lack of Christian social action.' 'The beginning of the nineteenth century saw a widespread interest in simple, vigorous and outward-looking religion. This attitude, known as Evangelicalism, affected all Protestant religious groups more or less and was at the root of many of the most important movements for social reform in the first half of the new Century. Among its particular triumphs may be noted the

suppression of slavery, largely the work of William
Wilberforce (1759–1833); the Factory Act of 1833 ...
educational reforms ... and the work of Lord Shaftesbury (1801–85), who achieved tremendous reforms in
mental hospitals, factory hours and conditions, the treatment of orphans, charity education, the safeguarding of
chimney sweeps' climbing boys and many other fields. It
would be no exaggeration to say that Evangelicalism
became the conscience of early Victorian England. Nor
was the effect confined to charity from above; it provided
the motive force for much of the early labour movement,
as seen in episodes such as the Tolpuddle Martyrs, and in
the careers of Labour pioneers like Keir Hardie and
George Lansbury.'[4]

The same commendation appears in Herbert Peacock's
book on British history for a similar period. Writing about
the effects of the Methodists, he says, 'They helped to
achieve a considerable decrease in drunkenness and
crime through their direct appeal to the ordinary people
and the example they set in their personal lives ...' 'It is
now clear that a great deal of working-class and trade
union activity had its origins in the Methodist communities of the industrial towns. The Methodists made a great
contribution to popular education and literacy ...'

Writing about the Evangelical Movement he notes:
'This movement within the Church is associated with the
important work of such men as William Wilberforce, the
Earl of Shaftesbury, Bishop Ryle of Liverpool, Granville
Sharp and Thomas Clarkson.' 'Wilberforce (1759–1833)
typified the evangelical approach to religious and social
problems. He was converted to evangelism [he
presumably means evangelicalism] in 1784 when M.P. for
Hull. In conjunction with Thomas Clarkson, he cam-
paigned continuously against the slave trade and secured
its abolition by Britain in 1807. These two men also

became the leaders of the Anti-slavery Society established in 1823 and which led on to the Emancipation Act of 1833. Their associates became known as the 'Clapham Sect' from their practice of meeting in the houses of their supporters in that district, and they published the *Christian Observer* which carried on a constant campaign against public immorality, slavery, brutal sports (such as bull-baiting and cock-fighting), bad factory conditions, the harshness and brutality of the criminal code and the state of prisons. They advocated popular education, and Lord Shaftesbury became president of the Ragged Schools Union, a founder of the Young Men's Christian Association and the working men's institutes. He agitated for factory reform and succeeded in securing protection for badly exploited minorities, of which the most notable were the boy chimney-sweeps.'

'The effects of the Evangelical Movement were considerable. The Evangelicals stirred the conscience of the nineteenth century and much social reform is connected with them . . .'[5]

Such documentation in text books of our own day thrills the heart of those who would follow in their footsteps. The Reformation had similar effects, the ripples of influence and benefit extending to the whole culture. Writing about the influence of the Reformation, Francis Schaeffer points out that it 'not only brought forth a clear preaching of the gospel, it also gave shape to society as a whole – including government, how people viewed the world, and the full spectrum of culture'.[6]

Spurgeon's Tabernacle – social concern nearer our own time

C.H. Spurgeon is best known for his fine Bible-based, God-honouring preaching to the converted and to the uncon-

verted. Few people, however, are aware of the vast army of
workers who shared the work of God at the Metropolitan
Tabernacle in London. None could doubt that the unique
position of preaching was maintained. The worship of the
Lord's people each Lord's Day would be the highlight of
church life together. But through the week the premises
became alive with activity. Arnold Dallimore has conducted some new research into the life of Spurgeon and he
says, 'The Metropolitan Tabernacle was not, as some have
assumed, merely a highly popular preaching centre. It was
not a church whose people largely came in from some
miles around and, after listening to a marvellous exercise
in Christian oratory, returned to their homes and seldom
thought about the place again till the following Sunday
morning. The Tabernacle was a great, working church.
The vast majority of the members lived in the heavily
populated area of London south of the Thames, and many
were so near they could walk to the services . . . there were
activity and work that brought great numbers to the
Tabernacle on many occasions during the week.'[7]

The premises were in use every day from first thing in
the morning (7 a.m.) to last thing at night (11 p.m.). By
1880 the church had established sixty-six distinct ministry
groups based on the church. These included the Pastor's
College, the Almshouses, the Orphanage and the Colpor-
teurs' Association. 'There were also several less prominent
institutions: the Evangelists' Association, the Country
Mission, the Home and Foreign Working Society, the
Loan Tract Society, the Sermon Loan Society, the Maternal Society, the Police Mission, the Coffee House Mission,
the Loan Building Fund, the Christian Brothers' Benefit
Society, the Flower Mission, the Gospel Temperance
Society, the Female Servants' Home Society, the Blind
Society, the Ladies' Benevolent Society, the Tabernacle
Evangelistic Society, and the Spurgeon's Sermon Tract

Society.'[8] Church members also organized Sunday Schools and ragged schools, and were involved with about forty 'mission' churches throughout London.

The church successfully amalgamated evangelism and social care and at the same time provided countless opportunities for Christian service. Some ministries were distinctly evangelistic. Others were distinctly of the nature of social care. Still others were a combination of the two. The Ladies' Benevolent Society 'met there in a sewing circle to make clothes for the children of the orphanage, for poor people of the congregation, and for other needy ones of the area'. The Maternal Society ladies gathered to prepare gifts for expectant women and then went to help them when they became mothers. 'Flowers were gathered at the Tabernacle by the Flower Society, and after being made into attractive baskets and bouquets they were taken to the homes of the sick and to hospitals. Mrs Spurgeon maintained a Bible nurse at her own expense, and other such nurses also functioned from the Tabernacle.'[9] With no state health visitors or social workers, and surrounded as they were by appalling conditions – filthy slums, over-crowding and poverty – the church responded in many tangible forms. The influence Christians exerted upon that immediate area of London was colossal.

An optional extra?

Is social concern leading to social action an optional extra, or should it be an integral part of church life?

Commenting upon the clear social implications of Isaiah 58:6–7, Dr Leupold says, 'Social suffering, wherever it is found, is to be relieved as much as lies in our power.'[10] Later, referring to verse 10 and the call of God to extend their 'soul to the hungry and satisfy the afflicted soul,' he writes, 'To expect God to hear our cries when we will not let the cries of the poor reach our heart is quite unreasonable.'[11]

Pessimistic caution!

R.B. Kuiper makes a point which few Christians would challenge: 'In evangelicalism the heart of the gospel must, of course, be foremost, but its social implications may not be ignored.'[12]

Fearing the social gospel of the modernists Christians have tended to over-react. A polarization has occurred. The modernist has a genuine concern for the physical, emotional and intellectual well-being of people but has no real gospel of salvation through the Christ of history and of the Scriptures. The evangelical has tended, over more recent years, to major on the spiritual salvation of individuals without saying or doing much about the social evils of the day. Must we be forced into this polarization? Is social concern inversely proportional to spiritual concern? Are we faced with an either/or situation or can we find a true balance?

The need for balance

Three areas of responsibility vie for the church's attention, time and resources: firstly, pastoral care for the people of God (worship, preaching/teaching, fellowship, prayer and counselling), secondly, evangelism and, thirdly, social concern. Each local church has to balance its life and labours so that these three major duties are adequately addressed. Maintaining the biblical balance between these three will take thought, planning and prayer. At times these areas overlap, often merging inextricably. Not one of the three should be neglected if we are to be faithful to our Lord. We are to make disciples of the nations through preaching the gospel and teaching the Word of God. But if we are to be true to the practice and teaching of Christ and his apostles we shall also need to care for the physical and mental well-being of our fellow men.

The need for revival

Two further obstacles to social concern need to be removed. In the first place brethren may read the foregoing history in quite a different way. All are agreed that the beneficial effects of the religious awakening of the eighteenth century and its impact on the nineteenth century indicated the glory of God working in and through his church. Some, however, believe that the church can only be motivated to social concern when there is revival. (Usually a concern for 'revival' means more than a revivification of the church, but is a heartfelt cry to God for the Holy Spirit to operate on a grand scale once more in our society – convicting of sin and converting thousands to faith in Christ.) The view is expressed that a new spiritual awakening would not only convert sinners but change society as well. Then, and only then, it is felt, would the transforming influence of Christianity be expressed in all areas of our society. Thus, with this approach, the danger is to pass over present social responsibilities and concentrate entirely upon spiritual exercises. 'Revival' becomes both the key for transforming an inactive and inadequate church and the panacea for social ills.

Wonderful as it would be to experience a widespread powerful activity of the Holy Spirit, we cannot wait for such large-scale movement before we demonstrate social care – just as we cannot wait for such a movement of the Holy Spirit before we preach evangelistically to sinners. That God works on occasions in an intensified manner does not obviate our social duties towards others at all times.

Has the church been squeezed out?

The second obstacle to social concern which must be dislodged is the prevalent feeling that the church has entirely lost its foothold in society. The historians Parker and Reid give support to this view. Having outlined the considerable good done to society as a whole by evangelicals, they note the decline of religion as it began around the beginning of the twentieth century. Commenting upon the First World War, they write, 'Many people found they could not believe in a God who could let such things happen – or, more simply, they were just shocked out of their conventional habits of mind and realized that they had never believed in anything at all.'[13]

Parker and Reid then outline the period of increased materialism as the standard of living rose rapidly. With this rise in prosperity there was coupled a rise in apathy towards Christianity. They continue: 'The Church seemed unable to cope with this apathy; its traditional roles in education, the care of the poor and the social services had been taken away from it by the state and it found difficulty in adjusting to the position of a private, voluntary body.'[14] Has the welfare state really pushed out the church from its caring role in society? Today we have more opportunities than ever for loving involvement in the community. Most churches have more openings than they know how to meet. The authorities cannot provide the depth of love, the self-sacrificing interest and concern, the Christian compassion and voluntary care that the church of Jesus Christ can provide.

Unconverted people deriving benefit from the church

In the parable of the mustard seed, 'birds of the air' nest in the branches of the well-formed church tree. There are unbelievers within most Christian congregations who are there, not for any good spiritual reason, but for the 'perks'. They derive support, practical help, financial assistance or just plain old-fashioned friendship from the church. They hear the Word preached evangelistically and are sometimes impressed, though not savingly. Christ anticipated these 'birds'. He foresaw those who would gain from Christian labour, love and life and yet would remain distinct from and outside of the true (spiritual) church. They bring their own peculiar problems.

Sunday School teachers and youth leaders have laboured year after year with such 'birds'. Teachers and leaders have one overriding aim, to share the love of God so that the youngsters come to faith in Jesus Christ! However, some of these 'birds' may be as ravens, driven by Satan to snatch the seed and successfully rob others of the benefit of the preached Word! (Matthew 13:4,19.) Others will be as hawks and one day turn and savage the church. Others will be like sparrows who know where to turn for help, shelter or food, or like starlings, out for all they can get. Some, God willing, will become nightingales who will soar to the spiritual heights and sing praise to God from believing hearts. And then what a glorious transmutation – from bird to branch, to become part of the living tree of the church of Christ!

References

1. R.C.H. Lenski, *The Interpretation of St Matthew's Gospel*, Augsburg Publishing House, p. 529.
2. R.C. Trench, *Notes on the Parables of our Lord*, Macmillan and Co., p. 315.
3. Francis A. Schaeffer, *The Great Evangelical Disaster*, Crossway Books, p. 116.
4. M. St J. Parker and D.J. Reid, *The British Revolution 1750–1970*, Blandford Press, p. 375.
5. Herbert L. Peacock, *British History 1714 – Present Day*, Heinemann Educational Books, p. 412.
6. Schaeffer, *Great Evangelical Disaster*, p. 22.
7. Arnold Dallimore, *Spurgeon – A New Biography*, Banner of Truth Trust, p. 153.
8. *Ibid*, pp. 153–154.
9. *Ibid* p. 155.
10. H.C. Leupold, *Exposition of Isaiah*, Evangelical Press, vol. 2, p. 287.
11. *Ibid*, p. 289.
12. R.B. Kuiper, *God-Centred Evangelism*, Banner of Truth Trust, p. 167.
13. Parker and Reid, *British Revolution 1750–1970*, p. 379.
14. *Ibid*.

15

Mobilizing the church

When one man is pastor, preacher, evangelist, social worker and politician it is no wonder that the church loses its sense of direction and little is achieved!

The objective facing the church is to present the love of God in a practical, as well as a propositional form. We must practise Christian love as well as preach it. Our desire is to bring sinners to faith in Christ. Such a desire will only be fully realized through the personal dedication of individual Christians. The expansion of the church requires the enthusiasm and commitment of God's people to yield themselves and their time to God. It is only as 'every part does its share' that there is 'growth of the body for the edifying of itself in love' (Ephesians 4:16). This growth will be expressed in two different forms. There will be the internal growth of the church, that is growth in 'the grace and knowledge of our Lord and Saviour Jesus Christ' (2 Peter 3:18), and there will also be external growth of the body as new believers are added to the Lord and to the church (Acts 5:14).

Over the past fifteen to twenty years there has been a renewed emphasis upon what is popularly called 'body ministry'. This aptly describes the functioning of the members as they make their individual contribution to the good of the church (Romans 12:3–8; 1 Corinthians 12:12–27; Ephesians 4:16). The re-emphasis upon this aspect of church life is to be welcomed. It is, however, one thing to be made conscious of this teaching in Scripture and yet another matter to try to encourage such functioning within the local church.

Realizing the potential

Every Christian loves to hear a success story. When churches are blessed, invigorated and enlarged all God's people who hear of it rejoice. Pastors eagerly read, or listen to, accounts of unusual progress and expansion in the hopes of learning something which will revolutionize their own local church. In the foreword to the book *The Church Unleashed*, Vernon Grounds writes about a church in this way: 'It's a fellowship that within ten years has been transformed from a small, stagnant in-group into a pulsating task force of vision, service, enthusiasm, and growth.'[1] It seems that everyone in that church is involved in some activity or other and few people have time for complaints or grumbles. There are fulfilment, growth and contentment in the service of Christ. What is their secret? It seems they have discovered how to release and realize the potential of the whole church! The central challenge comes halfway through the book: 'Any pastor could shape a church within five years if he: (i) stayed under the authority of Scripture; (ii) allowed the Holy Spirit to lead; (iii) loved the people; (iv) developed a clear-cut strategy . . . ; (v) communicated effectively.'[2]

The overall impression given is that every church is just bursting with members who would love to work for the Lord if only they were given the opportunity. Is this really the case? Are pastors really hogging all the jobs? Do they greedily snatch every responsibility, take on every duty and fulfil every ministry, resolutely refusing to let the rest of the church be involved?

It is more accurate to say that the vast majority of pastors are grossly overworked. They are expected to minister the Word of God three or four times each week, to be available for any enquiry, from anyone, at any time of day or night, on questions ranging from the heating system to the issue of demon possession; to visit every member of the church regularly; to visit all the sick, whether they have a sore throat or pneumonia; to be on the spot for the delivery of cement or oil; to work the duplicator, fix the organ, sit on boards of governors, be present at every activity and meeting on church premises and to evangelize the whole neighbourhood! The mentality of the 'one-man ministry' has swept the churches. Whether the pastor is stopping the membership functioning effectively, or whether the church membership is lazy and indifferent, something has to be done to mobilize the whole church!

Every man to his calling!

The apostles resolutely refused to be side-tracked from their main work of 'prayer and the ministry of the word' (Acts 6:4). Pastors need to insist upon their churches appointing others to share the pastoral care of the church. Deacons also need to be appointed. This means looking out 'men of good reputation, full of the Holy Spirit and wisdom' (Acts 6:3) who will be spiritual enough and wise

enough to get on with their work without constant supervision (or interference), from pastors. Every member has
to be faced with the dual challenge: 'What is your
contribution to the effective working of the body?' and
'What are you doing to further the cause of Christ?' For
the purposes of our present study it is the second
question which will receive our attention: 'What are you
doing to further the cause of Christ?'

Excuses for inactivity

The excuses for inactivity are many. One of the favourite
reasons expressed in order to evade the challenge to
evangelism is having the wrong type of personality.
'Evangelism needs an extrovert,' they say, 'and I am quiet
and shy.' Is it really a matter of temperament? Evangelism in its widest context is simply caring for people
with a view to sharing the love of God with them. There
are a thousand and one jobs which demand a quiet, gentle
disposition with a willingness to 'be' and 'do', rather than
'say'. (How the church can fulfil its responsibility to
provide opportunities and promote projects in which all
believers can function will be considered in detail later.)
Once converted a Christian can no longer use his personality as an excuse. As Dr Brandt stated, 'You can use
your background as an excuse for present behaviour only
until you receive Jesus Christ as your personal Lord and
Saviour. After that you have a new power within you that
is able to change your conduct.'[3]

Another excuse is that of inferiority, either real or
imagined. You will remember that Moses tried to hide
behind an excuse of inferiority. The Lord graciously
provided assistance for Moses, though it was clear the
Lord did not consider such help to be necessary (Exodus

4:14–16). We must not expect a similar solution, as there were special reasons for Moses being given such assistance. Believers must learn to overcome this particular problem and other weaknesses by concentrating upon personal strengths. No Christian is without gifts and graces from the Lord. Every believer has a contribution to make to the effective functioning of the church (Romans 12:4–6; 1 Corinthians 12:6–7,12; Ephesians 4:16). A clear-sighted view of one's own contribution is necessary. Such a personal assessment will be heavily dependent upon the objective assessment of the church. More often than not it is our brethren and sisters who see and understand our gifts and graces better than we do. Personal exaggeration is to be avoided at all costs. There is the exaggeration which undervalues and also an exaggeration which overvalues our personal contribution to the work of Christ. Paul exhorts the Romans: 'For, I say, through the grace given to me, to everyone who is among you, not to think of himself more highly than he ought to think, but to think soberly, as God has dealt to each one a measure of faith' (Romans 12:3).

God can overcome all our weaknesses! Writing about the fruit of the Holy Spirit in Galatians 5:22–23, Tim LaHaye concludes: 'The Holy Spirit-filled temperament does not have weaknesses; instead it has nine all-encompassing strengths. This is man as God intends him to be. It does not matter what one's natural temperament is; any man filled with the Holy Spirit . . . is going to manifest these nine spiritual characteristics. He will have his own natural strengths, maintaining his individuality, but he will not be dominated by his weaknesses. The nine characteristics of the Spirit will transform his weaknesses.'[4]

Lethargy

C.H. Spurgeon had strong words to say about inactive

Christians: 'An idle and barren Christian who is also Spirit-filled is a conception foreign to the New Testament and untrue to all experience.'[5] Believers must be faced with the demands of Christian commitment. Evangelism is not just a matter of personality, opportunity, talents or time. It is an attitude of mind and heart! It should be a priority for *every* Christian. Somehow, in some way, each believer must contribute to the ongoing development of the church of Christ.

A lack of evangelistic fervour is caused by:

1. A lack of love for the Lord.
2. A lack of love for people.
3. Laziness and indiscipline.
4. No sense of direction from church leaders.
5. A restraining influence from church officers.

Coupled with these is procrastination. Procrastination is one of the greatest enemies of evangelism. 'Procrastination is the thief of time.' The word 'procrastinate' is the combination of two Latin words meaning 'for' and 'tomorrow'. To procrastinate means to defer, to put off taking action; to make promises or resolutions, to decide upon a course of action and then delay their realization. There is sense in the saying: 'Do not put off until tomorrow what can be done today.'

Evangelism is a great subject for procrastination. It becomes the object of discussion and debate among Christians – the right conditions, the right moment, the right approach. Endless discussion; little action!

God commissions each of his children, 'Son, go and work today in my vineyard' (Matthew 21:28). And Christians have answered, 'I go, sir' (v. 30). Yet procrastination, deferring, putting off, has resulted in their not going. Those workmates you intended inviting to the meetings, those neighbours you resolved to speak to and befriend, that visit you were determined to make, that letter you planned to write . . . Evangelism is action. God has given his commission: 'Go!' We have replied, 'I go, sir' and by God's grace, we are to go!

There is work to do!

The Christian church is the God-ordained agent of evangelism. The Master has said to his servants, 'Go out into the highways and hedges, and compel them to come in, that my house may be filled' (Luke 14:23). Go to the blind, the lame, the sick, the deaf, the poor and outcast, the hopeless and helpless. But go also to the bank manager and government official, the professor of theology, the middle class, the self-employed, the nobility. Go to a Nathanael, a Nicodemus, a Cornelius, a Simon Peter, a James and a John, a Lydia, a Dorcas, an Apollos, a Sergius Paulus, a common jailer.

It is a great work in which to be involved. There are variety, excitement and pleasure in serving Christ by seeking to reach others. We shall meet with hindrances and suspicion. Roy Joslin warns of the problem: 'The weeds of ignorance, prejudice and fear will need to be uprooted so that the good seed of the gospel can be planted properly. The mental blockages of error, distortion and sentiment must be broken down before the foundation of truth can be laid.'[6]

How do we motivate those who make promises but do not fulfil them, like the son who answered, 'I go, sir,' but did not go? (Matthew 21:30.) It is quite clear that God does not appreciate unfulfilled promises (Ecclesiastes 5:4–5).

He has strong words to say to the lazy and indisciplined. Some of the most graphic of such expressions come in the book of Proverbs, for example:

> 'Go to the ant, you sluggard!
> Consider her ways and be wise,
> which, having no captain,
> overseer or ruler,
> provides her supplies in summer,
> and gathers her food in the harvest'
>
> (Proverbs 6:6–8).

The ant needs no constant supervision, no perpetual goading to force her to labour. Frank Tillapaugh writes, 'It is sad to see pastors trying to motivate their people with fear, ought-to, or you'll-be-blessed motivations. God uses want-to motivation because that is the only kind of driving force which works for any length of time.'[7]

There is a popular notion perpetuated in some Christian circles that a task must be unpleasant and totally unsuited to us for it to be clearly God's will! There is so much fear of selfishness and carnality that a strange mentality is produced. The thought runs in this way: 'The only way to be certain concerning the will of God is for it to be downright disagreeable to us!' Now, while selfishness and carnality are problems against which we are constantly to battle, it still remains that the Lord gives the 'will' to do. The motivation of believers comes by the internal operation of the Holy Spirit making us willing. 'For it is God who works in you both to will and to do for his good pleasure' (Philippians 2:13). God causes his people to be willing volunteers (Psalm 110:3). The willingness for any particular task will be based firmly upon love for God and his Christ. Love to God is the great motive behind all God-honouring work. All the works and labours of which we are capable are spoiled if we do not retain our 'first love' (Revelation 2:2,4). We love him and that affects our attitude to the saved and the unsaved. It motivates a desire for the well-being of saints and for the conversion of sinners. We love him because he loves us (1 John 4:19). His love to us conforms us to his will. It is 'the love of Christ' which 'constrains us' (2 Corinthians 5:14). So much so that we long no longer to live for ourselves but entirely for him!

Our spur to evangelism is the love which the Lord Jesus Christ demonstrated towards us in dying in our place upon the cross. That single act constantly stirs our hearts to love him and to further his kingdom in obedience to his command. He promised all the necessary resources and the needed power from heaven by the indwelling of the Holy Spirit (Acts 1:8).

Commitment is costly

When Saul was confronted by the Lord Jesus Christ on the Damascus road he reacted with the question: 'Lord, what do you want me to do?' (Acts 9:6.) Charles Bridges in touching upon the relationship between God's grace and man's obedience writes, 'Shall we then indolently wait until he works? Far from it. We must work, but in dependence upon him. He works not without us, but with us, through us, in us, by us; and we work in him. Ours is the duty; his is the strength. Ours the agency; his the quickening life.'[8] The church needs gospel partners and prayer partners but not sleeping partners! The idea that a man can be a member of a church and only attend worship, doing nothing for the edifying of the body, has to be brought to an abrupt halt. Professing believers who have no evangelistic zeal are to be questioned as to their true spiritual state!

Pastoral problems arise in churches because believers are basically self-centred. They ask, in effect, 'What can others do for me?' 'Why won't my husband be more loving?' 'Why won't my children show more understanding to me?' 'Why doesn't my wife respond to my needs for recognition, support and love?' And in respect to the Lord they say, 'Why has God let this happen tó me?' 'Why doesn't God do something to change my circumstances?' Life is viewed with 'self' at the centre. Much of modern-day evangelism has been based upon this basic self-centredness: 'You can be happier.' 'You can be more fulfilled.' 'Get high with Jesus.' Even, 'You can have your sins forgiven!' So it is not at all surprising that after conversion this basically selfish outlook is perpetuated. The emphasis of such thinking and preaching is completely wrong. Almighty God is in the centre of his creation (Revelation 4:2–4). He is Sovereign Lord. We have the privilege of being brought into his holy presence 'through the blood of the everlasting covenant' (Hebrews 13:20) and we have the high duty to serve him. The first question in response to God's overtures is 'What must I do to be saved?' (Acts 16:30) The second is, 'Lord, what do you want me to do?' (Acts 9:6.)

Equipping the saints

Christ gives men to his church who will be able to 'equip the saints for the work of ministry' (Ephesians 4:12). This commission to teach and train the church for its God-ordained role must be taken seriously. Each member has to discover what contribution he/she can make to the good of the whole and then go ahead and make it. Mobilizing all the church to multi-faceted ministry is the urgent need of the hour. Multiplication of workers, viewed from a human perspective, is a key factor in church growth and evangelism. The analogy of the body is ideal. Hendriksen comments: 'Just as the human body, when properly supported and held together, experiences normal growth, so also the church, when each of its members supports and maintains loving contact with the others and above all with Christ, will, under the sustaining care of God . . . proceed from grace to grace and from glory to glory.'[9]

Strategy and vision

In 1 Chronicles 12 an account is given of the gathering together of the great army of David, 'like the army of God' (v. 22). Men came from all quarters who were skilled in many different forms of warfare. There were 'mighty men, helpers in the war, armed with bows, using both the right hand and the left in hurling stones and shooting arrows with the bow' (v. 2), and 'mighty men of valour, men trained for battle, who could handle shield and spear, whose faces were like the faces of lions, and were as swift as gazelles on the mountains' (v. 8). Men came in their thousands who were 'equipped for war' (v. 23), skilful, brave and with undivided loyalty (v. 33).

In the midst of these fighting men were the children of Issachar 'who had understanding of the times, to know what Israel ought to do' (1 Chronicles 12:32). Vision, strategy and organizational skills were as essential as the mighty fighting force.

Whether the vision comes from pastors or deacons or from a clear-sighted member of the church is immaterial. It should not be assumed that a pastor, whose expertise lies in his handling of the Word of God in teaching and counselling the saints, will always be the one to see where the church can make inroads into 'enemy' territory.

Pastors are, however, responsible to provide the necessary training. A careful plan will take into consideration the resources available within the membership. Looking for gifts, skills and talents demands that leaders become more acutely aware of the potential within their church. If there is true spirituality, coupled with a real zeal to serve the Lord and a realization of the demands and responsibilities involved in a particular ministry, then training can follow. Classes, conferences, courses, seminars, books and tapes are readily available. There are many ways of drawing upon supplementary help from outside where the teaching and training required for a particular ministry goes beyond the capacity and ability of a local church.

For far too long the church has settled for second-best. The standard has been appallingly low. Examples easily come to mind. The average church magazine is often badly duplicated, with ghosting and smudges, sometimes the ink is so faint as to be illegible. The quality of the writing would often fail 'O' level English. The material itself is banal and uninspiring – being more like a gossip rag than a stimulating piece of Christian journalism. Tape recordings produced by churches are often of such bad quality as to be embarrassing. Why must we make do with shoddy work? Almighty God is worthy of our best! 'Whatever your hand finds to do, do it with your might' (Ecclesiastes 9:10). The Lord would have us make the most of every opportunity. When every department of the church, every effort at outreach and all church communications are of the highest possible quality the Lord God is honoured, and the world will begin to take us seriously. Generally speaking there are too few people doing too many jobs with the result that most of the work is done badly! The body of Christ should be composed of experts! Every member should try to be a specialist in his/her role and produce a good standard of work and perform the task at the highest level. Leaders should look for those who can be trained to do an even better job than they are doing: 'The greatest challenge a leader faces is to train others who can, from a human perspective, go on to do a better job in the ministry than he.'[10]

Our main problem is that of getting believers involved in specific ministries. The needs in the church and the colossal needs in the community about us require the mobilization of the whole church. When eyes are opened to the world around it will soon be evident there are many jobs to do. An evangelizing church is a caring church. Members of a caring church spend time with people in the community.

Women and paid employment

When considering the effective functioning of all church members we must recognize that a major problem faces the church at this present time. We are seeing a rapid rise in the number of women going out to work in paid employment. This is by no means a peripheral issue to the question of church growth and evangelism.

When a wife spends a considerable time at the office, factory, or school it is understandable that she expects a full participation by her husband in all household chores. The time that would have been available for church work and evangelism, by both of them, is greatly curtailed. The pressure upon women to go out to work in paid employment is very strong. Walter Chantry's challenging pamphlet sets the scene graphically: 'Our world sets its wares before women: Look at the money you can make! A paycheque is an immediate and tangible reward for labour. Look at the influence and respect you can command in a successful career! There is fun and excitement in the work

world – the social stimulation of interesting people, the
excitement of travel, the glamour of attention from others,
the intellectual challenges, and so on. But in reality these
often prove to be the baubles of Vanity Fair.'[11] The wife
and mother who is 'just' a housewife is intimidated, belittled and made to feel inferior. 'Does your wife work or is
she a housewife?' is an offensive insinuation. One does not
need to be a supporter of the feminist movement to react to
such careless and hurtful questions. To be a wife, mother
and a homemaker (Titus 2:5), together with caring for
others in the church and in the community, is the highest
of callings.

Married women in paid employment are, more often
than not, motivated by worldliness. Concern to maintain a
high standard of living, live in an expensive house, run two
cars, take holidays abroad and provide 'the little extras'
has swept so many Christian wives back to work. The
results of this widespread return to work are enormous.
Large-scale unemployment among men and young people
could be reduced instantly if married women stopped
taking their jobs. Children would be much more secure if
'mum' was at home providing the backbone for the family.
'There is no more pitiful person in the world,' writes
Walter Chantry, 'than the woman who "has it all together"
in business but whose family has fallen apart. She is the
epitome of energy, organization, talent, and efficiency –
only her children have not turned out well.'[12]

Being a wife and mother is probably the most important
and exacting task in the whole of society. There is the
demanding period when the children are small. Psycho-
gists are agreed that the early years are the most important
in a child's development. As the children grow up there is
no more exacting work in all the world, no more awe-
inspiring job description than being a godly mother: nurse,
counsellor,   confidante,   teacher,   guide,   psychologist,

friend, supporter, cook, cleaner, model-maker, artist . . . Add to that the role of a wife: help-meet, companion, confidante, partner, friend and lover and the role becomes more demanding. But there is yet far more involved in being a woman. There is the duty of ministering to the needs of God's people – the demands of Christian hospitality, washing the feet of the saints (sometimes required literally) and relieving the afflicted (1 Timothy 5:10). Beyond the bounds of the fellowship she is able to 'extend her hand to the poor' and reach 'out her hands to the needy' (Proverbs 31:20). Loving concern in the community is a prerequisite to effective evangelism.

Some of the finest gospel work recorded in Scripture was performed by women. The energies, talents and resources of our womenfolk are being channelled into shop work, factory work and office work instead of church work and gospel work. Work in paid employment, by our sisters in Christ, is killing the evangelistic movement of the church! If a woman derives satisfaction from being a wage earner, let her consider the greater reward which comes to those who minister in the service of Christ. It is tragic that women have been 'put down' and made to feel inferior. The reaction of so many has been to prove their equality or superiority in the business world and this has only multiplied our problems. The gifts and energies of a wife and mother are to be directed towards the home, the church and the community. They are to serve the Lord in a different setting from men. Their unique contribution is invaluable. Many godly women in the New Testament Scriptures used their skills for the service of the Saviour and they were not inferior to men in any way whatsoever.

As Donald Macleod states, 'The women whose acquaintance we make in the writings of Paul and Luke were not downtrodden and illiterate. Lydia, Priscilla, Phoebe, Lois, and Eunice, were ladies of intelligence, information, culture, resourcefulness . . .'[13] They were the equals of any man!

Both men and women in Christ need to accept their God-ordained position in the body. 'If the whole body were an eye, where would be the hearing? If the whole were hearing, where would be the smelling? But now God has set the members, each one of them, in the body just as he pleased' (1 Corinthians 12:17–18). John Eadie expresses the point like this: 'The body derives its vitality and power of development from the head . . . The church has a living connection with its living Head, and were such a union dissolved, spiritual death would be the immediate result. The body is fitly framed together and compacted by the functional assistance of the joints. Its various members are not in mere juxtaposition, like the several pieces of a marble statue. No portion is superfluous; each is in its fittest place, and the position and relations of none could be altered without positive injury.'[14]

> 'I heard the voice of the Lord saying:
> "Whom shall I send,
> And who will go for us?"
> Then I said, "Here am I! Send me"

(Isaiah 6:8).

References
1. Frank R. Tillapaugh, *The Church Unleashed*, Regal Books, p. 4.
2. *Ibid.*, p. 110.
3. Quoted by Tim LaHaye, *Spirit Controlled Temperament*, Kingsway Publications, p. 16.
4. *Ibid.*, p. 55.
5. Percy O. Ruoff, *Personal Work*, p. 26.
6. Roy Joslin, *Urban Harvest*, Evangelical Press, p. 8.

7. Tillapaugh, *The Church Unleashed*, p. 131.
8. Charles Bridges, *A Commentary on Proverbs*, Banner of Truth Trust, p. 224.
9. William Hendriksen, *Ephesians*, Banner of Truth Trust, p. 203.
10. Tillapaugh, *The Church Unleashed*, p. 107.
11. Walter J. Chantry, *The High Calling of Motherhood*, (pamphlet), Banner of Truth Trust.
12. *Ibid.*
13. Professor Donald Macleod, *Banner of Truth* Magazine, No. 81, 1970.
14. John Eadie, *Commentary on the Epistle to the Ephesians*, Zondervan, p. 324.

—— 16 ——

Strategic planning

The apostle Paul was a great 'planner'. He had vision and drive. He had received a commission from the Lord Jesus Christ himself (Acts 26:15–20) and he used his intellectual powers to plan, and then to execute, his strategy. Some Christians are of the opinion that it is unspiritual to formulate a strategy for evangelism, or indeed to plan for anything in church life! This was certainly not the view of the early Christians, as can be seen from the record of the apostles. When writing to Titus, the apostle Paul instructed his young assistant to meet him at Nicopolis, adding, 'for I have decided to spend the winter there' (Titus 3:12). Again Luke records other decisions which the apostle made: 'We sailed from [Mitylene], and the next day came opposite Chios; the following day we arrived at Samos and stayed at Trogyllium; the next day we came to Miletus. For Paul had decided to sail past Ephesus, so that he would not have to spend time in Asia; for he was hurrying to be at Jerusalem, if possible, on the Day of Pentecost' (Acts 20:15–16).

As an apostle in the early Christian church Paul knew

times when he experienced extraordinary leadings. Acts
16 records an example: 'Now when they had gone through
Phrygia and the region of Galatia, they were forbidden by
the Holy Spirit to preach the word in Asia. After they had
come to Mysia, they tried to go into Bithynia, but the Spirit
did not permit them. So passing by Mysia, they came down
to Troas. And a vision appeared to Paul in the night. A man
of Macedonia stood and pleaded with him, saying, "Come
over to Macedonia and help us." Now after he had seen the
vision, immediately we sought to go to Macedonia,
concluding that the Lord had called us to preach the gospel
to them' (Acts 16:6–10). Such a clear awareness of God's
will was not always the apostle's experience. He
sometimes made plans, even in awareness of the presence
of the Spirit of God, and then had to change them. While at
Ephesus, 'Paul purposed in the Spirit, when he had passed
through Macedonia and Achaia, to go to Jerusalem,
saying, "After I have been there, I must also see Rome"'
(Acts 19:21). But an evil plot caused Paul to change his
plans: 'he decided to return through Macedonia' (Acts
20:3). Again, when writing to the Christians at Rome he
shared with them an intention which had been on his mind
for a while: 'I do not want you to be unaware, brethren, that
I often planned to come to you (but was hindered until
now), that I might have some fruit among you also, just as
among the other Gentiles' (Romans 1:13). His planned
visit to Rome had been interrupted. So while the apostle
thought carefully through the development of his work,
and made plans accordingly, he was not so fixed in his
decisions as to be inflexible.

Built-in flexibility

What evangelistic possibilities could there be in a stinking dungeon in Philippi? Incarceration could have been seen as a serious setback to the apostle's plans but it was no interruption to the Lord's plans. The jailer was converted to Christ! The apostle Paul, that great evangelist of the Gentiles, saw the hand of God in the whole of his life. When again thrown into prison, this time at Rome, he writes to the Philippians, 'I want you to know, brethren, that the things which happened to me have actually turned out for the furtherance of the gospel, so that it has become evident to the whole palace guard, and to all the rest, that my chains are in Christ' (Philippians 1:12). Paul had not 'planned' a stay in prison in his evangelistic strategy – but the Lord had planned it for him! Persecution or imprisonment are to be viewed in the light of God's purposes. Everything is to be seen in a spiritual perspective. As with Joseph, years before, Paul would have been able to say, even in the most testing circumstances, 'As for you, you meant evil against me; but God meant it for good, in order to bring it about as it is this day, to save many people' (Genesis 50:20).

Hindrances may come from Satan as he works through his servants in the world. But 'There is no wisdom or understanding or counsel against the Lord' (Proverbs 21:30). God has the last word – and it is always the best! When Pilate arrested Jesus he foolishly supposed he had the Christ in his power. After some hours of interrogation the Lord kept silence. 'Then Pilate said to him, "Are you not speaking to me? Do you not know that I have power to crucify you, and power to release you?" Jesus answered, "You could have no power at all against me unless it had been given you from above"' (John 19:10–11). The devil can only do what the Lord permits him to do!

It is the Lord who has the overall strategy in hand. Consequently, even when our plans have been made carefully and prayerfully we 'ought to say, "If the Lord wills, we

shall live and do this or that"' (James 4:15). An example
of this attitude is shown when the apostle Paul departs
from Ephesus: 'I must by all means keep this coming feast
in Jerusalem; but I will return again to you, *God willing*'
(Acts 18:21). It is a great comfort to know that while 'there
are many plans in a man's heart, nevertheless the Lord's
counsel – that will stand' (Proverbs 19:21). It is the Lord's
purpose which will be established!

Planning requires consideration of the circumstances,
analysis of the issues, assessment of resources, reflection
upon possible approaches, discussion as to best methods
and setting the proposed steps in order. 'Not that we are
sufficient of ourselves to think of anything as being from
ourselves, but our sufficiency is from God' (2 Corinthians
3:5). 'A man's heart plans his way, but the Lord directs his
steps' (Proverbs 16:9). 'A man's steps are of the Lord; how
then can a man understand his own way?' (Proverbs
20:24.)

Counsel from the Lord

The Bible throughout teaches the providence of God in
theory and demonstrates the providence of God in practice. God 'works all things according to the counsel of his
will' (Ephesians 1:11). As the prophet Jeremiah cried out.
'O Lord, I know the way of man is not in himself; it is not in
man who walks to direct his own steps' (Jeremiah 10:23).
Derek Kidner expresses the thought in this way: 'For all
his freedom to plan, man only, in the event, advances
God's design.'[1]

One of the prophetic names for Christ is 'Counsellor'
(Isaiah 9:6). And a name given to the Holy Spirit is 'Par-
aclete' (John 14:16,26) which has a breadth of meaning
embracing Helper, Comforter, Advocate and Counsellor.

The Lord anticipates our need for advice and direction from him. Indeed, he requires it of us! To know God's mind is crucial. He alone has the overall strategy to hand. At the Jerusalem Council, when the apostles and elders had debated the issues relating to the conversion of Gentiles and their incorporation into the church, they concluded by sending out a letter to the Gentile converts, in which they used a telling expression: 'It seemed good to the Holy Spirit, and to us . . .' (Acts 15:28). There was no question of a vote with a 75% majority carrying the day. For 'it pleased the apostles and elders, with the whole church . . .' (Acts 15:22). The church was of a mind, but there was also a firm belief that they acted in accord with the Holy Spirit!

Once the need for a strategic approach has been accepted the areas of ministry must be clearly identified.

A point of contact

Whether our work is as evangelists seeking to establish a new gospel church, or as Christians concerned for evangelism from our local church, we are all searching for a point of contact. A desire for the spread of the gospel should cause us to be on the look-out for openings. Frank Tillapaugh makes a suggestion: 'We need to ask ourselves as we move about the city, Who are these people? What is their contact with the gospel? Is there something God would have me do?'[2] The question of utmost importance is, 'How do I make contact with these people so that I can share the love of God with them?' It is no longer sufficient to put on a 'gospel meeting' and hand out invitations. Few people respond to this approach these days. Nor is it satisfactory to waylay folk on the streets and challenge them, charging them with sin and insisting upon repentance!

Such a confrontation causes offence and dishonours the Lord.

What ways are there, then, in which we can reach out to our unbelieving neighbours, workmates, friends and family?

Meetings

'Gospel' meetings have tended to be too much like Christian services of worship, whereas the two activities ought not to be mingled. We need much more flexibility in our approach to the unconverted if we are to take our example from the New Testament evangelists. Paul reasoned, argued, discussed, debated, confounded, refuted . . . The emphasis is certainly upon dialogue. Evangelistic preaching has tended to get away from its New Testament roots. An uninterrupted monologue (1 Corinthians 14:30–31) is appropriate for Christian worship, though even here an opportunity for questions by the brethren appears to have been available (1 Corinthians 14:35).

Lectures on Christian doctrine designed for explaining a particular teaching to the unconverted/unconvinced have a limited appeal. However, meetings specifically designed in which no hymns are sung, no prayers offered and no collection taken may be of benefit to the person who is agnostic or a 'seeker'. C.H. Spurgeon wrote, 'All men are not alike indifferent; in fact, there are some persons who seem to have a sort of religious instinct, which influences them for good, long before they have any real love for spiritual things.'[3] We may expect some folk to be interested in talks on doctrine, though, of course, interest in theological issues is not the same as a desire for spiritual truth!

While meetings which have 'religious' subjects are

unlikely to attract many people there are a number of topics which will be of interest to a much wider audience. Social issues, when viewed from a Christian perspective, make a useful contribution to the church's impact on the world. There are some excellent Christian speakers who are highly qualified in a variety of disciplines. Many non-Christians will listen to a speaker who is professionally trained and competent. Issues like abortion, euthanasia, education, ecology, creation and evolution, human rights, racial understanding, cultural conflicts, depression and stress, can be presented from a biblical standpoint. While the intention is not to bring the subject round to the gospel, it is hoped that there will be a bridge built for further consideration. Thousands in our land have no awareness of the relevance of Scripture to normal everyday issues. To present people with a viable Christian alternative to the insipid humanistic stance at present in vogue will pave the way for later evangelism.

Meetings which present the biblical teaching on marriage, divorce and remarriage, the family, the role of husband and wife, bringing up children, the problems and pressures of adolescence, caring for elderly relatives and related topics have a relevance to those with whom we live and work. Bringing people to an awareness of the wisdom and compassion of God, as revealed in the Scriptures, lays a good foundation for later discussion about the God *who is*! (Hebrews 11:6.)

Luncheon clubs

A luncheon club designed for elderly persons could provide a substantial meal with opportunity to relax and enjoy good company. At the close of the meal, and as an integral part of the whole event, a speaker could address the gathering upon such subjects as 'The Dignity of Human Life,' 'Coping with Loneliness,' and 'Elderly does not mean Useless!' The object would be lovingly to confront the elderly with a sense of their own value and worth and to show how essential it is that the Lord God should have the prime place in their lives.

Other luncheon clubs could be arranged for businessmen where the subjects could be, 'Business Ethics in the Modern World,' 'Manliness,' 'Management Skills and Respect for Others,' 'Conjugal Trust,' 'Sexual Perversions and Their Cure,' and 'Work and Home.' Again the intention would be to present the data eminating from the Word of God, all founded upon a distinctly biblical ethic though not necessarily using Bible quotations.

Young mothers

A useful ministry to mothers of young children could be to provide a competent children's nurse from the congregation to run a playgroup-cum-nursery for one day a week. Commencing at 10 a.m. the mothers would leave their offspring in capable hands and have coffee together, with an opportunity for an informal chat. Before a buffet lunch a speaker could introduce a variety of relevant subjects. Older Christian women have a duty to train young women 'to love their husbands, to love their children, to be discreet, chaste, homemakers, good, obedient to their own husbands . . .' (Titus 2:4–5). There is great breadth of scope in these issues. Stimulating and challenging material should be presented in an interesting way. Following lunch the mothers could be free to do some shopping and return mid-afternoon to collect their children. A day's programme of this nature demonstrates Christian love and concern, presents clear biblical teaching and provides a bridgehead between the church and the world. Practical friendship expressed in this way will, God willing, lead to useful conversations about the Lord and make attendance at specifically evangelistic meetings that much easier.

An invitation to dinner

A large proportion of the population enjoy going out for a meal. There is still a certain appeal in being invited to a dinner where there will be a speaker. Such meals are often associated with grand occasions like banquets and the possibility of 'Mr and Mrs Average' being invited to one of these is most unlikely. When Christians take a little time and trouble to prepare attractive and palatable food in conducive surroundings the environment is transformed from the rather awe-inspiring ethos of a church service into a relaxed setting which ordinary non-church people find 'normal'. An appropriate speaker at such a gathering will do much to break down barriers existing in the minds of the unconverted. If such a gathering can remove the intellectual blockage and cause the unconverted to begin thinking seriously about the Lord God, it will have achieved untold good.

The gap in thinking between the world and the church is ever widening, as a newspaper article made clear: 'Today, at a generous estimate, seven out of ten of our people are outside the orbit of organized religion, and it should be plain that here we have a problem which should over-whelmingly be the main preoccupation of the churches. Today, alas, it is not only that these men and women don't come to church. It is also that whole masses of them know practically nothing of the facts of Christ's life, about the meaning or manner of worship, about sin and redemption.

With all their magnificent qualities of courage, endurance,
and good humour they have lost God, by which I mean
that contact with Him has no place in their lives, nor has
His authority any influence over their conduct.'[4] The situation is even more astounding when it is realized that this
article appeared in the *British Weekly* of 6 December 1945!
What further rapid deterioration has taken place in the
ensuing years! Couple this with the entry of large numbers
of persons from other lands bringing with them their own
religions and practices, and the confusion in society is of
immeasurable proportions.

Work with overseas students

The value of evangelistic work among students from overseas is brought out by Frank Tillapaugh: 'Frequently, the
international student is from the middle or upper classes
of a country where the gap between rich and poor, the
privileged and the powerless, is very great. The likelihood
that such a student would ever be contacted by Christian
missions in his or her own country is so small as to be
almost negligible. Missionaries are not usually able to
effectively contact the upper levels of society in such a
country, even if they are allowed entrance.'

'Almost any country you can think of is represented here
today by its young people, its future leaders. Some of
them, contacted by Christians taking a special interest in
their welfare, will return with a knowledge of the gospel.
What better world view could they take back home than
one based on the revelation of Christ? This represents a
challenging missionary potential for any local church. Dr
Mark Hanna of Biola College calls it "The Great Blind
Spot in Missions Today."'[5]

Dr Kuiper stressed a point which has a very real bearing

on missionary strategy. He wrote that 'A native evangelist may be expected to be more influential with his as yet unsaved neighbours than a foreign missionary can be.'[6] The hours spent by European missionaries in language learning and trying to understand a new culture abroad might be better spent in this country evangelizing foreign students. It was not accidental that in the apostle Paul the Lord chose a man who had a thorough working knowledge of three languages and three different cultures. As far as the biblical record goes, it would seem that Paul worked in the areas where he fully understood the language and culture of the people. Missionaries may have a zeal for the Lord and for the lost, but the present emphasis may not be the best way to use talent and energy. In other words, gospel work overseas needs a thorough evaluation and a 'strategy'!

To return to the question of evangelizing students in Britain, how do we set about reaching students – either those from the United Kingdom or those from overseas? The best means is through personal friendship. Strangers often receive a cold or even semi-hostile reception in this country. When Christians take a genuine interest in students it will break down barriers and lead to openings for sharing Christian truth with them. Furthermore, learning about other countries through a 'living representative' is far more interesting than any geography lesson.

The value of personal contact

The strength of evangelism often lies in existing relationships or the establishment of new personal relationships. An encounter with the Philippian jailer led to his family being converted (Acts 16:33–34). With Lydia of Thyatira her conversion led to the conversion of her household (Acts 16:15). New converts have to be instructed as to their immediate duty to live for the Lord and to speak of him when appropriate. John Miller puts it in this way: 'Should you have the privilege of leading a person to faith in Christ, it is important that you stress to him that the Holy Spirit's immediate goal for his life is a highly visible public confession of Christ before his family, among his friends, on the job and in the church of God.'[7] There are those converts who react spontaneously, like the woman of Sychar who spoke to the men of her city, which resulted in a number of conversions (John 4:28–29,42). No matter how slight the contact and how few the words, great good may be achieved. And while few contacts will be as obviously blessed as when Philip met the Ethiopian Minister of Finance (Acts 8:26–39), none should be regarded as useless. When a Christian has a spirit for evangelism he is excited by the endless possibilities by which the Lord may begin to bring sinners to faith. The most insignificant of encounters may be, in the providence of Almighty God, the first step which leads ultimately to conversion.

Telephone counselling

A twenty-four hour telephone counselling service is time-consuming as it requires manpower for many hours of unfruitfulness just waiting for phone calls. However, a service could be provided to the community whereby those with specific problems would be able to ring during a fixed period on, say, two evenings in the week. Emergencies are catered for by the Samaritans' telephone service, so the church could be available to give help and advice in specific areas such as marriage counselling, family counselling, drug abuse and alcoholism.

However, dealing with these problems will require great wisdom, spiritual strength and perception. Our hearts should go out to the victims who are suffering as a result of the widespread breakdown of morality and order. These are fellow human beings made in the image of God. They have a God-given dignity even though they are unconverted sinners. How can we hope to convince them of the love of God if they do not experience the love of God's people? Where people are hurting the church must care and take what action it can!

Peripatetic evangelism

Considerable numbers of young people frequent the streets in our cities and towns, not only in the daytime and evening, but also through the night. To get alongside them is a dangerous work requiring a special talent. Those who attempt this work would do well to obtain training. There are excellent courses run in 'detached youth work' where the skills and disciplines learned can easily be adapted to Christian work. But, as the Saviour warned his disciples, 'Behold, I send you out as sheep in the midst of wolves. Therefore be wise as serpents and harmless as doves' (Matthew 10:16). The need for wisdom promotes earnest prayer to God! (James 1:5.)

Literature

R.B. Kuiper gives a superb illustration of the way in which the Lord sometimes uses literature: 'When by the direction of divine providence someone left a tract at a certain house in England, God had it planned that Richard Baxter (1615–1691), having been converted through the reading

of that tract, would write *The Saints' Everlasting Rest*; that
Philip Doddridge (1702–1751), moved by the reading of
that treatise, would write the *Rise and Progress of Religion in
the Soul*; that William Wilberforce (1759–1833), under the
spell of that work, would write his *Practical Christianity*; and
that Thomas Chalmers (1780–1847), founder of the Free
Church of Scotland, profoundly influenced by that book,
would develop into one of the greatest preachers of all
time, whose sermons were to be published two years after
his death in twenty-five volumes.'[8] What countless
thousands have been helped into the Christian way and
along the Christian path by these four worthies? And who
left that first tract? What greater honour could a believer
experience than being the agent in such a development? In
God's purposes, one inconspicuous, unknown saint
started a landslide of spiritual blessing.

The value of literature should not be assessed purely on
the number of persons who come to faith as a direct consequence of reading it. (It is always to be borne in mind that
the primary manner in which the Lord wills to present the
gospel and save sinners is through preaching – see Romans
10:17; 1 Corinthians 1:21.) There is, however; a wider use
for literature. Good literature, attractively presented,
serves to communicate, on a wide scale, the church's interest in the community, the assurance of welcome to all
visitors (a factor which cannot be taken for granted even in
our evangelical churches), and an implied willingness to
give rather than to beg. When folk are constantly harassed
by zealots on their doorstep it will make a change to receive
a gently worded, gracious communication from the true
church. Such material softens the ground for further
opportunities. In other words, there is much good will to be
gained from well-prepared pamphlets.

Three Nigerian Christians, working for their government on a three-month project in this country, wanted to

find a place of worship on the Lord's Day. They asked the hotelier, 'Where is there a gospel church?' Though not a Christian he had received literature and was able to give clear directions which linked these three saints with brothers and sisters for worship!

An attractive Christmas card/pamphlet (irrespective of our convictions regarding 25 December) will do much to circulate information. Generally we try to achieve far too much at one time. It is not necessary to put 'everything' into our leaflets! The quality of our presentation must be good. Poor material will definitely do more harm than good. In modern jargon it will be counter-productive! The advent of reasonably priced word processors and printers, coupled with inexpensive photocopying when producing large quantities, leaves the church without excuse. Why are we so slow to use modern technology for the service of the Master?

When telling that unusual parable of the unjust steward, our Lord drew a contrast between the attitude of the unsaved and that of the saved. He said, 'The sons of this world are more shrewd in their generation than the sons of light' (Luke 16:8). As Norval Geldenhuys points out, it was the Lord's objective 'to use the parable to call attention to the "wise" and diplomatic manner in which worldlings generally act towards their fellow men in order to achieve their own selfish aims. In contrast with the diplomatic, clever conduct of such people, those who are members of the kingdom of light too often act unwisely and undiplomatically towards others. Instead of behaving in such a manner that they bind others to themselves, they act so that people are unnecessarily repulsed.'[9]

Radio ministry

What has been said about literature is equally applicable

to radio work. In assessing the usefulness of Christians being involved in local and national radio the criterion is not how many come to faith as a direct consequence of one particular broadcast. This type of attitude is characteristic of Christian 'head-hunters' who want to be able to count 'scalps' and report successes in their prayer letters and meetings! By means of radio and television we are able to present an alternative to the effeminate cleric and the pious hypocrite so often shown to represent Christianity. Courses are available for those Christians who have the basic gifts to learn the skills necessary for broadcasting.

A strategic approach

'Strategy' is concerned with the art of war. It is the management of an army in a campaign. The church of Jesus Christ is at war with the world. Our only permitted weapon for attack is 'the sword of the Spirit, which is the word of God' (Ephesians 6:17). Wielding this sword can be done in a variety of ways. We have to be more adventurous, more flexible, more outgoing! The potential for diverse action is within the churches. Our resources have to be assessed, directed, utilized so that we obtain the maximum benefit for the cause of the gospel. But evangelism is not the only concern facing the church. Nor would I wish to give the impression that it is the major work. The different areas of responsibility and working need to be understood and the relationship between each section clearly defined. The diagram on pages 238-9 gives a simple example of how church life can be viewed and structured. Members are then faced with the challenge as to their particular area of service. Christians working to a planned approach based on the principles of Scripture, carefully orchestrated, not only produce a greater efficiency and effectiveness but also create, within the fellowship of saints, a greater sense of interdependence and mutual respect.

References
1. Derek Kidner, *Proverbs*, The Tyndale Press p. 118.
2. Frank Tillapaugh, *The Church Unleashed*, Regal, p. 49.
3. C.H. Spurgeon, *The Soul-Winner*, Pilgrim Publications, p. 117.
4. Quoted by Percy O. Ruoff, *Personal Work*, IVP, p. 13.
5. Frank Tillapaugh, *The Church Unleashed*, pp. 171, 172.
6. R.B. Kuiper, *God-Centred Evangelism*, Banner of Truth Trust, p. 195.
7. John Miller, *Evangelism and Your Church*, Presbyterian and Reformed, p. 93.
8. R.B. Kuiper, *God-Centred Evangelism*, Banner of Truth Trust, p. 221.
9. Norval Geldenhuys, *Commentary on the Gospel of Luke*, Marshall, Morgan and Scott, p. 415.

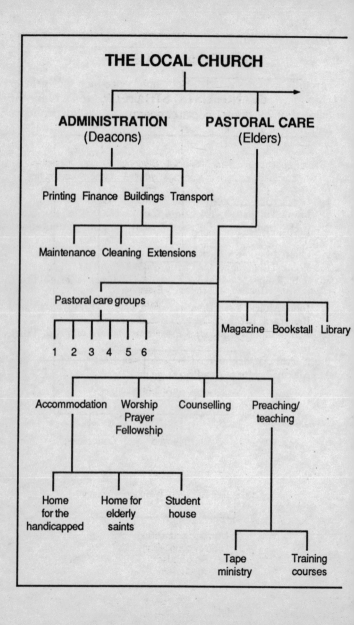

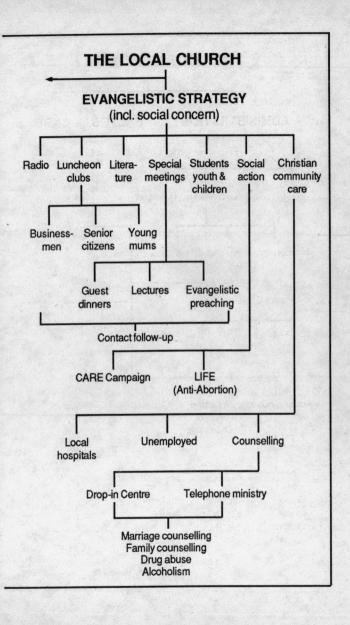

— 17 —

Persistence

The opportunities facing the church today are immense.
These are exciting times in which to live. There is clear
evidence that God is at work, with the resulting influences
of blessing for the saints and the conversion of sinners.
God-honouring worship is being owned by the Lord and
faithful congregations are experiencing 'times of
refreshing . . . from the presence of the Lord' (Acts 3:19).
When the church enjoys liberty and freedom in prayer,
God hears and answers according to his will. Furthermore, he is also able to work through the simplest
testimony and the living witness of the youngest of his
saints.

The emphasis of this book has been upon the living
dynamic of the individual Christian and each local
church. It is by so many ordinary means that the Lord
achieves his purposes and brings sinners to faith in his
Son. However, some planning is not only desirable but
also necessary. By means of the Scriptures the Lord
indicates the need and usefulness of men appointed as

evangelists. Larger churches will be able to support a man
from their own income, whereas smaller churches will
need to unite in a commitment to find the needed finance.
Nevertheless supporting evangelists is by no means the
full answer of our duty to 'disciple the nations'. Evangelism has to be planned and organized from the
churches. Strategic planning is required to capitalize on
the potential in the membership and to move into the
openings within the community. Michael LeRoy, in an
article entitled, 'Fighting On All Fronts,' makes this
observation of the church in the nineteenth century: 'The
strength of the period of Wilberforce and Shaftesbury was
that Christians operated at every possible level, through
the direct work of the church, prayer, and Christian
teaching, personal care, organized care, charities, campaigns, politics and Parliament.'[1] Today the church has
the resources and the manpower if they can only be
harnessed and directed. The opportunities lie before us
but so do the obstacles.

Satan the enemy of God

The old enemy of Christ and his church is actively
engaged in his pernicious work. When Paul eagerly
wanted to return with his companions to encourage the
Christians at Thessalonica he was thwarted by the devil.
Paul wrote to the saints, 'But we, brethren, having been
taken away from you for a short time in presence, not in
heart, endeavoured more eagerly to see your face with
great desire. Therefore we wanted to come to you – even I,
Paul, time and again – but Satan hindered us' (1
Thessalonians 2:17–18). When it comes to understanding
the wiles of the evil one we must not be 'ignorant of his
devices' (2 Corinthians 2:11). At times he comes through

open hostility by stirring up such hatred against the
Christian church that persecution breaks out; then he is
that great adversary who 'walks about like a roaring lion,
seeking whom he may devour' (1 Peter 5:8). At other
times he is far more subtle and disguises himself as a
friend of the fellowship. It is a fearful thought that 'Satan
himself transforms himself into an angel of light'! (2
Corinthians 11:14.) He has the world blinded to the truth
as it is in Jesus. 'If our gospel is veiled, it is veiled to those
who are perishing, whose minds the god of this age has
blinded, who do not believe, lest the light of the gospel of
the glory of Christ, who is the image of God, should shine
on them' (2 Corinthians 4:3–4). Against the power of
Satan the church is helpless, unless she leans heavily
upon him who will shortly crush Satan under her feet
(Romans 16:20). We must pray that 'the God who
commanded light to shine out of the darkness who has
shone in our hearts' will also shine in many more hearts,
'to give the light of the knowledge of the glory of God in
the face of Jesus Christ' (2 Corinthians 4:6).

Darkness hates the light

A further obstacle to evangelism is found in the resistance
of so many unbelieving people. There is in some a total
apathy. They do not care enough about religion even to
oppose it. They are not concerned what we preach, or
where we preach, for they have no interest whatever in the
matter. They have no thought of God; they care nothing
about him, or his service, they only use his name in
swearing and cursing. They are lethargic, indifferent folk.
These are the worst kind of sinner and unbeliever to reach
with the gospel. It is far better for a person to react
violently to our gospel than not to react at all!

Another obstacle we face is self-righteousness. A self-righteous person finds no room in his heart or life for the Lord Jesus Christ. He will not come to Christ because he is not conscious that he has any need of a Saviour. He does not seek to be forgiven for he has no awareness of any wrong or wickedness within him. He does not plead to be lifted up 'out of a horrible pit, out of the miry clay' (Psalm 40:2), because he does not know that he is a fallen creature who is 'dead in trespasses and sins' (Ephesians 2:1). Such people are impervious to the overtures of love in the gospel, because of their own self-righteousness. In arrogance and conceit they consider, 'If there is a God he will surely have ear-marked a place in heaven for me. Heaven just wouldn't be the same place without me!'

A further hindrance to the gospel is found in the utter worldliness of so many with whom we have to do. They have so many of this world's goods. They have their luxurious houses, their boats, parties, lavish entertainment, holidays abroad and just about all that money can buy. Their motto might well be 'Let us eat and drink, for tomorrow we die' (1 Corinthians 15:32). Worldliness can also be expressed in the obsession with which some people work. They will rise early, work late, neglect their families, neglect their health and ignore God. Such people are consumed by covetousness; their one aim is to be rich and influential. How can we hope to reach them with the claims of God and of his Christ?

The opposition to Christian evangelism is of gigantic proportions. Where is the believer who is sufficient for these things? When we cry out to the Lord, 'Who then can be saved?' the reply is still the same, for the Saviour answers, 'With men this is impossible, but with God all things are possible' (Matthew 19:25–26).

Unbelievers are heading for hell

Although we may be deeply thankful to God that no one he has purposed to save will ultimately be lost through our negligence yet it behoves us seriously to consider the plight of the unconverted. Whatever the manner in which sin expresses itself in their lives, whether through apathy, self-righteousness or worldliness, we are to remember, 'There but for the grace of God, go I.' 'The message of the cross is foolishness to those who are perishing' (1 Corinthians 1:18). And they are 'perishing'. Each day is for them a day nearer judgement and the subsequent punishment for eternity. The Bible doctrine concerning hell may not terrify the unconverted, but it certainly causes the converted to be sober and serious in evangelistic endeavours.

The power of the gospel

The apostle Paul was delighted at the privilege of being a minister of the New Covenant. In 2 Corinthians 3 he explained his understanding of this unique ministry. It is 'the ministry of the Spirit' (v. 8), 'the ministry of righteousness' (v. 9) and, by implication, it is the ministry of life! (v. 7.) In the fourth chapter he demonstrates his conviction concerning the power of this gospel ministry. Here is a confident note to encourage every Christian seeking to promote the cause of Christ through active evangelism. He writes, 'Since we have this ministry, as we have received mercy, we do not lose heart' (2 Corinthians 4:1). It is a great temptation to be discouraged by the relatively poor response we see to gospel endeavours. The danger is that we shall begin to lack confidence in the gospel itself, or to want to adjust the message to make it more palatable. 'But we have renounced the hidden things of shame,' writes the apostle, 'not walking in craftiness nor handling the word of God deceitfully, but by manifestation (open statement) of the truth commending ourselves to every man's conscience in the sight of God' (2 Corinthians 4:2). However depressing the response to evangelism may be, we must not adjust the content and deny or discredit the truths of God's Word. No hidden tricks are employed and no secret societies with their dark concealed initiation rites. Everything about the church – all its doctrines and all its practices – is open to the view of the world. We invite examination. Everything about God and his dealings with men is commendable. 'I am not ashamed of the gospel of Christ, for it is the power of God to salvation for everyone who believes' (Romans 1:16). What a privilege it is to be servants of such a God with such a gospel!

Promises and rewards from God

As we draw to a conclusion two stimulants to dogged determination in evangelistic work need to be considered. These are the promises and rewards of God. Gospel work is hard, laborious work. The battle is fierce and the issues at stake are monumental. We are in alien territory and the great enemy does not yield up ground easily. Impossible obstacles are to be overcome by the power of the Spirit of God. Evangelism takes time, for it is not a work to be rushed, but we are confident that God is busy doing his own work in his own way. He has promised that the Word will accomplish what he pleases and prosper in the things for which he sends it forth (Isaiah 55:11). He can work with us or he can work without us. Our responsibilities are limited; once the seed is scattered we can sleep soundly. The seed will sprout and grow, though we know not how (Mark 4:27).

Holding the precious promises

'Therefore, my beloved brethren, be steadfast, immovable, always abounding in the work of the Lord, knowing that your labour is not in vain in the Lord' (1 Corinthians 15:58).

'Let us not grow weary while doing good, for in due season we shall reap if we do not lose heart. Therefore, as we have opportunity, let us do good to all' (Galatians 6:9–10).

Such promises should spur us on in evangelism. How can we lose heart when we are promised a harvest if we persevere? Christians are involved in the greatest enterprise which has ever been undertaken. We are sharing in the construction of a cosmopolitan church. The people of God will be drawn from all sections of the community and all corners of the earth. Something of the great variety of people was reflected in the early Christian church. There were 'fishermen, merchants, artisans, farmers, tax-collectors, city and village dwellers; Pharisees, Sadduccees, scribes and Zealots; Palestinian and non-Palestinian Jews; ignorant and learned men; Hebrew and Hellenistic Jews; priests and laymen, etc., etc.'[2]

The breadth of the church company is expressed in the apostle John's experience as recounted in Revelation: 'After these things I looked, and behold, a great multitude which no one could number, of all nations, tribes, peoples, and tongues, standing before the throne and before the Lamb, clothed with white robes, with palm branches in their hands, and crying out with a loud voice, saying, "Salvation belongs to our God who sits on the throne, and to the Lamb!"' (Revelation 7:9–10.) This is not just a cosmopolitan church in terms of nationalities or races, but also in respect of cultures and subcultures. To be involved in such growing work is a great blessing in itself. Christian evangelism is demanding, often inconvenient and time-consuming. But it is the most rewarding work in the world.

Having an eye to the rewards

To look to the reward is by no means unspiritual. Moses turned his back upon all the treasures of Egypt because he judged 'the reproach of Christ greater riches . . . for he looked to the reward' (Hebrews 11:26). There is a reward in this life as we experience tranquillity and inner peace from God; there is a reward in faithfully fulfilling our duty towards God and there is a reward yet to be given in the world to come.

What will really count when we get to heaven? As Paul writes to Timothy, 'We brought nothing into this world, and it is certain we can carry nothing out' (1 Timothy 6:7). In terms of possessions, as the context makes plain, this is absolutely true. But there are some things which we can take with us. We can be 'rich towards God' (Luke 12:21). Our goods will perish and our empires will fall, but some things will last. Our spiritual fruits of evangelism will be with us. What a welcome such brothers and sisters will give us in glory! Furthermore when believers are faithful to God in the exercising of their gifts and the grasping of opportunities the Lord will reward them. The greatest of all rewards is spoken of by the Master in the parable of the talents: 'So he who had received five talents came and brought five other talents, saying, "Lord, you delivered to me five talents; look, I have gained five more talents besides them." His lord said to him, "Well done, good and faithful servant; you were faithful over a few things. I will make you ruler over many things. Enter into the joy of your lord"' (Matthew 25:21). Commendation from the Saviour is the greatest of all rewards. To hear him say, 'Well done, good and faithful servant,' surpasses all honour and praise in this world. It is more precious than all the gold and silver on earth. This is the reward of greatest magnitude. Look, too, at the blessing which follows, for the Master says, 'Enter into the joy of your Lord.' 'For the joy that was set before him' he 'endured the cross, despising the shame' (Hebrews 12:2). What holy contemplation gripped the Saviour's soul as he considered the 'fulness of joy' that there is in the presence of the Father! (Psalm 16:11.)

When we have sacrificed our time, energy, money and the praise of the world, when we have prayed and struggled with the Lord and pleaded and exhorted sinners to come to Christ, we shall, at best, have done no more than was our duty. We shall say, 'We are unprofitable servants. We have done what was our duty to do' (Luke 17:10). It is to God alone that all glory belongs!

> 'God be merciful to us and bless us,
> And cause his face to shine upon us.
> That your way may be known on earth,
> Your salvation among all nations.
> Let the peoples praise you, O God;
> Let all the peoples praise you.
> Oh, let the nations be glad and sing for joy!'
> (Psalm 67:1–4.)

References
1. Michael LeRoy, 'Fighting On All Fronts – Charity versus Politics', *Third Way*, vol. 9, No. 8, August 1986, p. 25.
2. Eric Wright, *Tell the World*, Evangelical Press, p. 79.